DAVID BUICK'S MARVELOUS MOTOR CAR

The men and the automobile that launched General Motors

Lawrence R. Gustin

"A meticulously researched book written in a popular style that's difficult to put down. By skillfully weaving together the careers of David Buick and his contemporaries and their car, Larry Gustin fills a gaping hole in automotive history."

David L. Lewis, professor of business history, University of Michigan

"If the question is Buick-related, Larry Gustin has the answer. He's also an entertaining story teller and accomplished wordsmith."

Don Sherman, technical editor, **Automobile** *magazine*

"Gustin offers new insights into the largely unknown and often-tragic life of David Dunbar Buick, a significant but neglected figure in the early automobile industry of Michigan. He also shows how the intertwined work of David Buick, Billy Durant, Walter Marr and Dallas Dort resulted in a very successful Buick Motor Company, which led to the creation of General Motors. This is a 'must read' for anyone interested in the early history of Buick, General Motors and Flint, Mich."

Charles K. Hyde, professor of history, Wayne State University

"The phrase, 'It's now or never,' explains the drive behind this work on David Buick. Larry Gustin has studied the person, his work and the characters involved in the David Buick drama for decades. In this book, he has brought all that research material into sharp focus. The interests of automotive history are well served by this welcomed work."

Leroy Cole, past president, Society of Automotive Historians

"Larry Gustin has at long last brought us the long overdue story of a forgotten automotive pioneer. And he has done it in a manner that only a writer with a lifetime interest in the history of the Buick automobile could ever hope to accomplish. It's about time."

Terry B. Dunham, president, The Buick Heritage Alliance

Symbolic of the revolution in transportation early in the 20th century, a Buick Model 10 "White Streak" motors past a team of oxen on a bridge near Standish, Mich., circa 1908.

DAVID BUICK'S MARVELOUS MOTOR CAR

The men and the automobile that launched General Motors

by
Lawrence R. Gustin

Buick Gallery and Research Center, Alfred P. Sloan Museum

For Rose Mary
For Bob and Wendy; David and Jennifer
For the grandchildren: Grant, Olivia Rose, Zachary

ISBN 0-9786269-0-7

Copyright © 2006. All rights reserved
Published by Buick Gallery and Research Center, Alfred P. Sloan Museum

Layout, Design, and Printing: *Signature Book Printing, Inc.*
www.sbpbooks.com
Artist: *Jeremy Brenn*

Contents

Buick general manager's message 7

Foreword 9

One: An interview in Detroit 17

Two: From Scotland to Detroit: The early years 21

Three: Gasoline engines: The obsession begins 29

Four: Buick and boats 39

Five: First Buick automobile 43

Six: Charles Annesley: Finding a missing link 57

Seven: 'Valve-in-head' engines 63

Seven sidebar: On engine technology, by Kevin Kirbitz 76

Eight: Buick starts a new company 81

Nine: Move to Flint 89

Ten: First Flint Buick 103

Eleven: The irrepressible Billy Durant 121

Twelve: Buick thrives, but where's the founder? 141

Thirteen: David Buick hits the road 153

Fourteen: Oil in California 159

Fifteen: The final years 175

Acknowledgments 209

Index 222

About Buick Gallery and Research Center 230

A word from Buick's general manager

Today, as we create new chapters in Buick's illustrious heritage with such outstanding models as Lucerne and others soon to come, it's a great time to reflect on the beginnings of the Buick marque more than 100 years ago.

Many automotive historians agree that Buick rightly claims one of the most important and dramatic chapters in U.S. automotive history. After all, the fact that Buick laid the foundation for the birth of General Motors is only part of its rich heritage.

Much of the credit for Buick's early success goes to William C. Durant, that master salesman, promoter and organizer who would later found General Motors. In his day, he was widely acknowledged as the auto industry's greatest leader. And in building Buick, he had a lot of help – people with now familiar names: Charles Nash, Walter Chrysler, Louis Chevrolet. And some with names not quite as familiar: Walter Marr, Eugene Richard, Harry Bassett and so many others. As Alfred P. Sloan Jr., GM's great leader of a later era, once said, "Buick had the management of stars."

But until now, not much has been said about the man who gave his name to the marque – David Dunbar Buick. He hasn't been entirely ignored because his last name has adorned about 40 million motor vehicles over more than a century. But he has gotten little attention because not much was known about him. With this new volume, that has changed. The author, Larry Gustin, who has spent decades researching Buick's heritage for such books as *Billy Durant: Creator of General Motors* (author, 1973) and six editions of *The Buick: A Complete History* (co-author, 1980-2002), was a newspaper reporter and editor for 25 years before he became Buick's assistant public relations director. Larry, who was honored with a 1999 Distinguished Service Citation from the Automotive Hall of Fame for his historical writing and other activities, recently retired. He tells the David Buick

David Buick's Marvelous Motor Car

story as it really happened.

David Buick and his motor car is no Hollywood rags-to-riches tale. There are plenty of bumps along the way. But here was a person who nursed his dream of building his own automobile into a reality. And by creating this automobile company and turning it over to Durant and others, he became an important figure in the birth of General Motors.

In 1994, when Bob Coletta, then Buick's general sales manager and later its general manager, dedicated a plaque at David Buick's birthplace in Scotland, he made this comment: "It is certainly appropriate for us to honor this man, not only because his name identifies our automobiles, but because his genius and hard work formed the beginning of an unsurpassed automobile success story – that is still being written."

The story *is indeed* still being written, and I see great things ahead for Buick. But if you want to know how it all started, here is where you'll find it.

Steve Shannon,
General Manager,
Buick Motor Division

"Mr. D.D. Buick is a gas engine expert and is very largely responsible for the creation of the marvelous motor which bears his name."

–William C. Durant, leader, Buick Motor Company, in a letter dated May 7, 1906. Durant would found General Motors in 1908 with Buick as the foundation.

"It was Buick that made any kind of General Motors car line worth talking about."

– Alfred P. Sloan Jr., GM's legendary chief executive after Durant, discussing the Buick marque's stature in the early years in his biography, *My Years With General Motors.*

Foreword

In any discussion of automotive history, Buick deserves special attention. That would be true if only for this: Buick was the financial pillar on which General Motors – which became the world's largest industrial corporation – was created.

But that's only part of it. Buick has produced a great deal of automotive lore. There were the innovations, starting early with the "valve-in-head" engine that surprised the auto world with its power and efficiency.

And famous models – Century, Roadmaster, Super, Skylark, LeSabre, Riviera, Gran Sport, Grand National, GNX, Park Avenue. And, okay, the 1962 Special with America's first mass-produced V-6, which, along with the turbocharged 1979 Riviera S Type, was proclaimed a *Motor Trend* car of the year.

Buick's concept car legacy begins with the legendary Y-Job, the industry's first "dream car," and includes XP-300, LeSabre, Wildcat, Centurion and up through the decades to the classic convertible Velite in the new millennium, a model almost everyone wanted produced.

There were notable styling features – boat tails, hardtop convertibles, hood ornaments with goddess and bombsight designs, "sweep-spear" bright metal side decorations, front fenders that swept back to touch the rear fenders, carnivorous pop-art grilles of the '40s and '50s, and – most famous of all – portholes. And great engines after the early valve-in-heads, including the "Fireball" straight 8, the so-called "nailhead" V-8 and the "3800" 3.8-liter V-6, also available turbocharged and then supercharged.

Buick's pioneer-era racing teams led by Louis Chevrolet and Wild Bob Burman won 500 trophies from 1908 to 1910, and Buick's stock block V-6s of the 1990s dominated several fields at the Indianapolis 500. Speaking of sports, golf and Buick linked up with the 1958 Buick Open that pioneered bringing major corporate sponsorships to sports. Later there were more Buick-sponsored PGA tournaments – with ads featuring Tiger Woods as a Buick spokesman.

International heritage? Buick's is, in a word, impressive. Before 1910, Buick was the foundation for GM Export and GM of Canada. A Buick in 1914 was the first car to cross South America. Adventurer Lowell Thomas used a Buick in 1923 for the first motor expedition into Afghanistan. Buicks swept speed, reliability and fuel economy awards in tests conducted by the Soviet Union in 1925. Also that year, GM Export sent a Buick Standard Model 25X around the world without a specific driver – passing the car from agent to agent – to prove the reliability of the car and GM's global network.

In the 1920s and '30s, Buick – the "Empire" car from Canada – was a favorite of British royalty. During King Edward VIII's abdication crisis, his fiancé, Mrs. Wallace Simpson, made her legendary escape to Cannes in a Roadmaster he had bought for her – and Edward himself owned a custom-built 90 Series Buick. In China, Buicks were big with business and political leaders from 1912 to World War II, including – recently confirmed – the last emperor, Pu Yi, and a postwar president, Zhou En-Lai. In fact Buick was so popular in China that when GM and China agreed on a $1.5-billion joint venture in Shanghai in the late 1990s, the Chinese insisted Buicks must be the first models produced. Soon Shanghai Buicks were leaders in the booming Chinese market.

Also internationally, a 1948 Special completed the second Pe-

Foreword

David Dunbar Buick

Leroy Cole

king-to-Paris rally (1997). The first was 90 years earlier, but this one went through Tibet. A 1949 Super wagon circled the globe, starting and ending in London, in "Around the World in 80 Days" (2000). That vintage-car rally commemorated the dawn of the new millennium. A 2002 Buick Rendezvous won a silver medal in the 15,000-mile Inca Trail adventure drive (late 2001). Lead driver Pat Brooks collected his award at a Buick-sponsored reception atop Rio de Janeiro's Sugar Loaf. International jeweler Nicola Bulgari displays his collection of about 50 vintage and modern Buicks in Rome (he has even more in the United States). He cruises in them with journalists for articles in classy European magazines.

The Buick name has been very visible in entertainment. Among many examples: A 1940 Limited Phaeton is in the famous airport scene with Humphrey Bogart and Ingrid Bergman in *Casablanca.* Tom Cruise and Dustin Hoffman drive a 1949 Roadmaster convertible across the country in *Rain Man*. Vintage Buicks are prominent in *Pearl Harbor* and *The Road to Perdition.* Stephen King places a 1954 Buick (but with a '53 mistakenly on the jacket) at the center of one of his horror stories, *From a Buick Eight.* It became a movie. And somewhere out there is the music video, *Aliens Ate My Buick.*

Buick was the starting (and growing) place for auto leaders from the beginning. Among them: William C. Durant, GM's founder; Charles W. Nash, a founder of what became American Motors; Walter P. Chrysler, founder of Chrysler Corporation; and Harlow H. Curtice, a postwar GM chief executive and *Time* magazine's 1955 "Man of the Year." Louis Chevrolet, onetime Buick racing star, helped Durant form Chevrolet Motor Company. Moving to recent times, Lloyd E. Reuss was chief engineer and then general manager of Buick before serving as GM president in the early 1990s.

What about David Dunbar Buick? When the story of the Buick automobile is recounted, its namesake typically is granted his several perfunctory lines of type. David Buick – or Dave, as he liked to be called – is remembered as a successful plumbing inventor. Sometimes he's even praised as a developer of fine gasoline engines in the pioneer days. But usually he comes off as a dreamer ignored and forgotten first by his company, and then by the public, and ultimately by auto historians.

It's true he's listed in the Automotive Hall of Fame. Get your name on roughly 40 million cars and you'll be there. But not much has been written about him. For one thing the slight but hard-edged Scottish immigrant (1854-1929) never recorded his accomplishments

Foreword

in any detail. His family didn't help – it didn't preserve many of his letters and photographs. He himself didn't attract positive attention with his later business ventures. And because he died broke, and therefore was labeled a failure, auto historians generated little energy filling in the blanks.

As one historian, George S. May, observed in his exhaustive 1975 book, *A Most Unique Machine: The Michigan Origins of the American Automobile Industry,* "few aspects of American automobile history have been so poorly recorded as that detailing the movement of David Buick from the plumbing business into the business of developing and manufacturing engines and automobiles."

But this much is known. David Buick led a team that created gasoline engines for motor cars that were truly remarkable. They were powerful, durable and efficient engines that proved formidable on race tracks and in hill climbs. And, more important, those engines provided the power to negotiate the deeply rutted mud, clay and sand roads that often defeated other cars in the early 20th century.

David Buick created one of two big story lines that connected in Flint, Michigan, in 1904. His theme was about a faltering little company with a great engine, Buick Motor Company. The other big story line was that of the brilliant organizer and promoter, William C. Durant. When Durant was introduced to the Buick automobile, it was almost like an explosion in the business world. That combination, Durant and Buick, formed the beginning of General Motors.

In the 1960s, '70s and '80s, it was still possible to learn about David Buick, Billy Durant and their times from a few first-hand sources. David's grandson, David Dunbar Buick II, well remembered the auto pioneer who had once lived with him and his family. Fred Hoelzle, who knew David just a little and who worked on one of the first Buick engines, lived into his 90s in the late 1970s and loved to discuss the early days. Also available in the early 1970s were Flint philanthropist Charles Stewart Mott, a General Motors board member for 60 years, who lived to age 97, and Durant's widow, Catherine, then in her 80s, both of whom had been witnesses to those early days when Durant took over David Buick's company and created a giant.

David Buick's Marvelous Motor Car

Aristo Scrobogna, Durant's last personal secretary, remembered in the 1980s that Durant talked about respecting David Buick's abilities. Charles E. Hulse, a Flint vintage car buff from the 1930s, related memories of his interviews with Walter Marr, who built the first Buick automobile, and others who were with Buick Motor Company from the company's earliest days. George H. Maines, a locally prominent public relations man, didn't know Buick personally, but recalled in the 1960s he had interviewed Durant about David.

For a few years now, or a few decades, I've been searching for David Buick. Back in the 1960s, as a young newspaper reporter and automotive editor in my hometown of Flint, I listened to George Maines, Sloan Museum Director Roger Van Bolt and local historian Clarence H. Young tell the true stories of David Buick, Billy Durant and the beginnings of General Motors in hours of fascinating conversations. In the 1970s, I spent many hours interviewing C.S. Mott and Catherine Durant about those early days for a biography of Durant. In the 1980s, I began two decades of employment at Buick public relations, becoming assistant director and semi-official company historian while updating five reprints of a Buick history book co-authored with Terry B. Dunham and first published in 1980.

In 1994, I journeyed to David Buick's old hometown in Scotland to help unveil a plaque near his birthplace. And on the occasion of Buick Motor Division's centennial in 2003, and the 150th anniversary of David Buick's birth in 2004, I applied (while at Buick PR) for a Michigan historical marker commemorating his achievements, and those of his company. The only state marker on the grounds of General Motors headquarters in Detroit, it's positioned along Jefferson Avenue facing Beaubien Street, five blocks down Beaubien from the original Buick engine shop of 1900. That shop was in a building that, at this writing, is still standing.

So in the early years of the new millennium, there were reasons to take a new look at the life of the founder of the Buick automobile. The story may always be incomplete. But while no new caches of letters and documents have surfaced to this date, one significant archive became available as this was being written. The research material

Foreword

of the late Charles E. Hulse, mentioned above, was made accessible through the courtesy of Hulse's daughter, Susan Kelley, vintage car enthusiast Jack Skaff and the Sloan Museum's Buick Gallery and Research Center. A number of changes were made based on Hulse's research. Also, new information became available about Charles G. Annesley, a 19th century link between Henry Ford and Walter Marr – and therefore between key figures in the birth, early in the 20th century, of Ford Motor Company and General Motors. This was thanks to Michael W. R. Davis, who shared his unpublished master's thesis on Annesley, an interesting but little-known figure.

The best way to deal with David Buick's life is as part of the larger and more dramatic story of the beginnings of the Buick automobile. While the record is thin, some of the significant pieces of new information combined with a careful re-examination of the available record makes it possible to build a more complete account of this man, against the backdrop of this period, than has been done to date. I received special help from the above-mentioned Terry Dunham, my co-author of six editions of *The Buick: A Complete History,* and from William B. Close, whose wife Sarah is a granddaughter of Walter Marr, Buick's first chief engineer.

Their contributions show up in the following. However, individuals may interpret similar information in different ways. Therefore, it's appropriate to state that I'm alone responsible for the opinions and errors that may have crept into these pages.

We're still searching for David Buick, but here, at least, is a starting point.

*** Lawrence R. Gustin***
Flint and Lake Orion, Michigan
Spring, 2006

Chapter 1

An interview in Detroit

Maybe he saw too much. Too many people making all the decisions. Too much chaos as the company expanded rapidly. Too much work, too many hours.

"When we were getting the Buick Motor Company under way, there wasn't an executive in the place who ever knew what time it was," David Dunbar Buick lamented in 1928. "We worked until we had the day's job done and were ready for tomorrow and then we went home – and not until then…."

"For seven years I didn't have a Sunday or holiday off – not even Christmas or the Fourth of July. I worked 12, 16, 18 hours some days…I tell you, the automobile business was a tough one in those days."

You can debate whether he was complaining or boasting. But David Buick was telling the truth. Said William Beacraft, Buick's first engine plant foreman and master mechanic: "I used to sleep in the shop, but we could never keep up with demand." All of the pressure did leave Buick, in his own words, "a physical wreck." So a little more than a year after William C. Durant, the super promoter, built up Buick Motor Company and then used its success to create General Motors in 1908, David Buick just packed up and wandered off.

Claiming illness from overwork and pocketing maybe $100,000 in severance, he left the company. Buick left Buick. In the spring of 1910, he put Michigan behind him and headed for California. He soon boasted of big wins in the oil fields there. But the success was illusory and short. Over the next several years, he apparently lost most of his Buick Motor Company nest egg. He followed with other business ventures that were also either failures or disastrous failures. When he stumbled back to Detroit, he was close to destitute.

David Buick's Marvelous Motor Car

David Buick through the years

In early 1928, an impoverished David Buick was tracked down at his workplace at the Detroit School of Trades by a young newspaper reporter named Bruce Catton, and consented to a rare interview. The 5-foot-5 ½ auto pioneer looked all of his 73 years. He was thin and frail and bent. He had a deeply lined face, coke-bottle glasses and wisps of gray hair barely covering his baldness.

He had not been easy to find. David Buick couldn't afford a telephone (let alone an automobile), so his name wasn't in the directory. "Time was when every city editor in Detroit knew where to find David Buick," Catton observed. "Today not one does." But Catton, a reporter for the Newspaper Enterprise Association, had his sources. He also had an historical bent – he would become the first editor of *American Heritage* and a Pulitzer Prize-winning Civil War historian.

Buick was at the school because he had found a low-paying job as an instructor and was glad to have it. Catton arrived eager for the interview because, as he positioned it, "in all the collection of strange tales that are told in Detroit, the automobile capital, there is no tale as strange as the tale of David Buick."

The tale is strange because Buick's name was famous, his accomplishments were significant and his fortune was nonexistent. That's what captivated Catton, but it was also strange because Da-

An interview in Detroit

vid Buick was hard to typecast. One acquaintance painted Buick as a rough-talking man, "always chewing tobacco." Another, Detroit businessman and politician John C. Lodge, who has a freeway named after him, labeled Buick "a hard man to do business with." When Enos DeWaters, later Buick chief engineer, arrived at the company in 1905, David Buick startled him with this greeting: "Well, I don't know what in hell you're going to do, so you might as well start as general foreman in the Assembly Department." In later years, a string of lawsuits in California tarnished his reputation at the same time they depleted his finances.

Yet Benjamin Briscoe Jr., a Detroit auto supplier and manufacturer, and briefly Buick's financial angel, described Buick as "a personal friend and a fine chap generally." His grandson, David Dunbar Buick II, told the writer his namesake was "quiet, a dreamer." Buick's surviving letters reveal a logical mind and a gentle disposition.

Another reason Buick's story is strange is because, for a long time, it was decidedly non-automotive. His early tinkering was in plumbing – he patented 13 plumbing inventions. In the mid 1890s, when Henry Ford and others began building horseless carriages, Buick was beginning to focus on making stationary and portable engines for the farm, and then he was on to powered boats. When he did catch the car bug, it brought him both great fame and great pain, almost simultaneously.

Intrigued, Catton sensed Buick was a man whose dimming memory still held a story. And so that day in 1928, they sat across from each other in a small room of the Detroit School of Trades, and began to talk about Buick's career.

Chapter 2

From Scotland to Detroit: The early years

For the true beginning, scroll back to Scotland. David was born September 17, 1854. He arrived in a small row house built of local red sandstone at 26 Green Street in Arbroath, a Scottish fishing village on the North Sea, the only child of Alexander and Jane Rodger Buik. (Note the spelling, and the footnote.)* He was baptized October 15 as a Presbyterian in the Church of Scotland.

All that exists of Green Street 150 years later is a bit of curbing along the front of the former Masonic Hall (sold in 2005 to the British Legion), a building more than a century old, where a plaque commemorating David Buick's nearby birthplace was unveiled in 1994. The street's other buildings were demolished in the early 1970s for a housing development.

But in 1851, when a census was taken, 297 people lived in 62 dwellings along Green Street. Most were employed in textiles. About half were locally born. The rest had come from other parts of Scotland, except for 21 from Ireland.

In 1851, Alexander, 20, was living with his parents on High Street in the nearby village of Forfar. Like his father, James, he was a carpenter. Jane Rodger, 17, lived at the nearby Salutation Inn, where she was a servant. But other Buicks and a David Dunbar lived on

---

* As another Arbroath native, Eric G. Buick, notes, Eric's ancestors also sometimes spelled it Buik. According to Eric, the spelling sometimes varied depending on what day it was and is of no significance. He said Jane's maiden name of Rodger was also often Roger. Other variants for Buick in Scotland include Bewicke and Bowick. Possible definitions range from bauk or baik, an unploughed ridge or wooden base, or the head rope of a fishing net. Or bouk or buik, which could mean bulk, size, quantity or the touchhole of a cannon. Or buik or buke or beuk, a book, record book or the Bible. A place in Northumberland is named Bewick, from the Old English beo + wic, meaning outlying farm, apparently a station for the production of honey.

David Buick's Marvelous Motor Car

David Buick's birth record in Arbroath, Scotland. Note the 'Buik' spelling.

Green Street in Arbroath, where the young couple moved after their marriage on May 22, 1853, in the Church of Forfar.

Arbroath was a prosperous community. At the harbor, trade was booming, though ships now faced big competition from a railroad. Some 2,750 tons of flax were landed from ships for processing in 1854 but 6,000 tons arrived by rail. A newly invented stone-cutting machine revolutionized a local quarry industry, according to local historians Eric G. Buick (no relation) and Alasdair M. Sutherland. Paving stone from Arbroath was soon found on the streets of New York and Cologne. Two Arbroath manufacturers had a stand at the Paris Exhibition where they sold one of their new lawn mowers to Napoleon III.

But there were threats. Men were posted on the outskirts of town to check all arriving travelers because a cholera epidemic had broken out in Montrose in 1854. Also the Crimean War was at its height, and recruiting sergeants regularly called on the town.

Ships left Arbroath for destinations around the world. *Storm Nymph,* for example, sailed for Melbourne, Australia, October 19, 1854, with a mixture of cargo and passengers. Cheap transportation

From Scotland to Detroit: The early years

out of Leith and Dundee was available to emigrants, who more often chose to travel from Liverpool and Glasgow. In the mid-1850s, favorite destinations were Canada and Australia. The United States was an unusual choice.

Arbroath was not only prosperous but visually interesting with small shops strung out along its picturesque harbor below the impressive ruins of Arbroath Abbey, where Scotland's Declaration of Independence was signed in 1320. But apparently it wasn't prosperous or interesting enough for Alexander. Two years after David's birth, Alexander took his little family to the United States, settling in Detroit, Michigan. The city was in the middle of a population boom, having grown from a frontier outpost of 2,200 in 1830 to a booming city of 45,000 in 1860. By 1890, Detroit would be a metropolis of 205,000.

In the mid 19th century, Detroit was an attractive city, with suggestions of its French beginnings still evident in its architecture and its people. The city fronts on the Detroit River, a wide and still beautiful blue-green strait connecting Lake Erie and Lake St. Clair. Detroit was a major stop for ships negotiating the St. Lawrence River to Great Lakes ports as far away as Chicago on Lake Michigan and – especially after the locks opened at Sault Ste. Marie in 1855 – Marquette and Duluth on Lake Superior.

Alexander was likely following other family members when he brought his family to Detroit. William Wolcott Buick, who lives in Pennsylvania, said his grandfather, a Detroiter named William Dunbar Buick, and whose parents were married in Scotland, was said to have been a first cousin of David Buick, "twice removed." The middle name of Dunbar and the Scottish heritage is enough to suggest the relationship. In the mid 1800s, there were several Buick families in Detroit.

In 1859, three years after the family's arrival, Alexander, 28, died. David was 5. Jane, age 26, was a widow with a young son in a new land. David would have to grow up fast. While he did attend the Bishop public school, he also helped out his mother by working a newspaper route – it's reported he delivered the *Detroit Free Press* and *Daily Union*. At age 11, David got mad at a teacher, threw an inkwell and jumped out a window, his grandson told the writer. He never returned.

Green Street in Arbroath, Scotland, where David Buick was born about halfway up the block on the left on September 17, 1854. This photo was taken 99 years later, with the street decorated for the 1953 coronation of Queen Elizabeth II. But small stone row houses along the street could date back a century. A plaque commemorating David Buick's birthplace was placed in 1994 on the building on left with the seven chimneys.

It was 1865, an emotional year. His mother, Jane, 32, married Daniel Wilson, 28, in Detroit on December 6 with David signing as a witness. (Jane, who would have a daughter with Wilson, operated a Detroit candy store for years). Also that notable year – the Civil War ended; Lincoln was shot – young David left Detroit to work on a farm.

Four years later, age 15, he was back, finding a job in Detroit at the Alexander Manufacturing Company, which made plumbing fixtures. Sometime in this period, by most accounts, Buick became an apprentice brass finisher in the James Flower & Brothers Machine Shop downtown. All kinds of brass and iron articles were manufactured there, using many types of machines. Young men learned skills they would need to prosper in Detroit's great industrial age that was beginning to muscle up. Among them: Henry Ford, an apprentice there a decade later, in 1879.

The shop's atmosphere was captured by Frederick Strauss, a sweeper there at age 12 when 16-year-old Henry Ford arrived.

From Scotland to Detroit: The early years

Buick & Sherwood, a major plumbing supplies business in Detroit by the 1890s.

Strauss's recollection, related by Sidney Olson in *Young Henry Ford,* was that it was a loud and raucous place: "It was a great old shop. There were three brothers in the company, all in their 60s or more… they were Scotch and believe me they could yell. They manufactured everything in the line of brass and iron…they made so many different articles that they had to have all kinds of machines, large and small lathes and drill presses. They had more machines than workmen in that shop…. Everything about the place was as old as the three brothers. The building was so old it was braced and shored up all over to keep it from falling down."

Buick learned well from the Flower brothers. He developed into an excellent brass finisher and eventually became factory foreman at Alexander Manufacturing.

The stories vary on how David Buick first became associated with William Sherwood. Some say they were old schoolmates, others that they met at the Alexander or Flower firms. In any event, they were friends as well as co-workers. In 1882, when the Alexander firm was failing, Buick and Sherwood took it over, turned it around and gave it their names. Buick later claimed Buick & Sherwood Manufacturing Company became the largest manufacturer of plumbers' supplies "of its kind" in the country. That was probably an exaggeration, but at least the company was big enough to make its owners moderately prosperous.

Besides his ability to work with brass and to lead a group of workers, David displayed a talent for invention. Between 1881 and 1889, he patented 13 plumbing inventions for a lawn sprinkler, flushing device, water closets, bathtubs, valves and the like.

His best-remembered success at Buick & Sherwood was also his most significant – developing a method of annealing porcelain to cast iron to create white bathtubs and other fixtures. Historians point out this process had huge commercial implications at a time indoor plumbing was booming. Buick could have become very wealthy by capitalizing on these desirable white fixtures. But it turned out that while he excelled in mechanical ability and inventiveness, David had poor instincts for success in business and finance – although for a time he seemed to do quite well.

Buick was 24 when he married Caroline (Carrie) Katherine Schwinck in Detroit on November 27, 1878. They began a family that would include four children: Thomas D., Frances Jane, Mabel (or Maybelle) Lucille and Wynton R. Their home at 373 Meldrum Avenue (1187 Meldrum today) in Detroit was likely a small two-story "gingerbread" style like a few nearby survivors. Today the site, on the west side of Meldrum between Lafayette and St. Paul, is vacant. Buick & Sherwood, at the southwest corner of Meldrum and Champlain (now Lafayette), was in walking distance, a half block away.

By the late 1890s, Buick seemed all set. He was regularly patenting his plumbing inventions and the business was doing well. He was raising a family. He was a prominent member of the Detroit Yacht Club and was racing sailboats with some success.

He also saw himself as something of a civic leader. Prominent citizens began coming forward with ideas on how to celebrate Detroit's 200th birthday in 1901. Buick was one of them, offering up a grand plan for a city monument, an icon "taller than any skyscraper" that would have "the outward appearance of a human figure." Buick was proposing a colossal statue of Cadillac – Antoine de la Mothe Cadillac, the founder of Detroit. It would measure 100 feet across at the shoulders and would house a museum, observatory, convention hall and other amenities.

The idea was ignored. Buick enjoyed the several bicentennial parades anyway, commenting particularly on one star attraction, "a very handsome woman of superb figure" who drew acclaim driving a Roman chariot.

But something else was also turning his head – the gasoline engine. As historian Arthur Pound observed in *The Turning Wheel: The Story of General Motors Through 25 Years*: "To David Buick a bathtub must have seemed a dead and inconsequential thing in contrast with the gasoline engines which had long engaged his eager and inquisitive mind." Or, as someone put it in shorthand, you can't drive a bathtub to town.

David Buick's Marvelous Motor Car

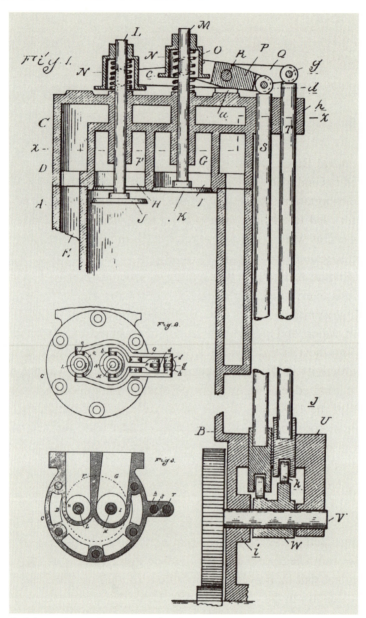

Buick engineer Eugene Richard included these drawings in his valve-in-head engine patent application in 1902. The early success of David Buick's automobile is largely attributed to the "marvelous motor" created by the Buick team, and so described by General Motors founder William C. Durant.

Chapter 3

Gasoline engines: The obsession begins

David Buick turned to gasoline engines at a dynamic time for inventors and machinists. The world was on the edge of a revolution in transportation. The enormous popularity of bicycles in the late 19th century led to advances in manufacturing of precision metal components, as well as creating a mindset for individual transport via a mechanical device rather than by horse.

Engine technology was rapidly advancing. Inventors and machinists everywhere experimented with steam, electricity and even springs as motive power. Internal combustion engines fueled by gasoline, vapors and natural gas were being invented and improved.

But most of this was happening in Europe. While horseless carriage activity in Detroit was beginning to stir, the city was not yet on the cutting edge of automobile technology – not even close. By the start of the 1890s, Europeans were well ahead of Americans, with some motor vehicle production already under way. The first American gasoline motor car was not driven until 1893. The first in Detroit arrived in 1896.

Actually, the first known automobile in Michigan did not come from Detroit, but from the little farming community of Memphis between Flint and Port Huron. It was steam powered, it was called "The Thing," and it was built in 1884-85 by Thomas Clegg and his father, John. Tom Clegg said The Thing could move along at 12 miles per hour and that he drove it about 500 miles total on 30 trips through farm country in the summer of '85.*

---

* When the writer visited Memphis in 1981 for a newspaper story about a state historical marker being placed there to commemorate The Thing, the city treasurer, Harold Fries, 74, could still remember seeing one of Tom Clegg's ancient steam vehicles rusting on a ridge. That was until one day in 1931, when Clegg's nephew

Clegg once complained, according to Arthur Pound, that his vehicle always returned to the shop under its own power, overcoming every grade and bog in its path, but could not overcome "the sneers and abuse" of public disfavor. In 1885, the people of Memphis and environs were not ready for the automobile.

Auto historians credit two events for accelerating interest among U.S. automobile enthusiasts – the World's Columbian Exposition of 1893 (better known as the Chicago World's Fair) and the *Chicago Times-Herald* auto race, the first American car race, also in Chicago, in 1895.

The Chicago fair was impressive, including, in no particular order, the first Ferris Wheel, a variety of gasoline engines, the "muscle dancing" of Little Egypt and one gasoline-powered vehicle – a quadricycle patented by Karl Benz of Germany. Among attendees were three men whose names would be remembered – Charles B. King, Ransom E. Olds and Henry Ford.

While Olds and Ford were mere visitors, King, a multi-talented 28-year-old Detroit engineer, was very much a participant at the fair. He won its highest award for a pneumatic hammer he had designed. A steam brake beam he had invented was also displayed – it would eventually become a standard item on rail cars. These significant inventions provided money for King's motor vehicle experiments.

King tried to get a vehicle ready for the 1895 *Chicago Times-Herald* race. He was unable to beat the deadline – but he was not alone. At one point an amazing 83 vehicles were entered; but on race day – Thanksgiving 1895 – only six made the starting line.

One was entered by J. Frank Duryea. Historians generally date the first successful drive of a gasoline-powered automobile in the United States to September 21, 1893, in Springfield, Mass., when

---

and another man pushed the historic vehicle over the ridge and into a swamp. "The machine disintegrated as it crashed down the hill," said Fries. "Mr. Clegg was mad about that. He said, 'What did you do that for? Henry Ford might have wanted it for his museum.' " Actually, Ford apparently did. He is said to have sought to move Clegg's small shop to Greenfield Village, but the request came several months after Tom Clegg had torn it down. Pieces of Clegg's old steam auto may still be sitting in the swamp at the bottom of the ridge.

Gasoline engines: The obsession begins

Above: Charles B. King (right) and assistant Oliver Barthel in the first gasoline automobile driven in Detroit, on March 6, 1896. Below: Henry Ford and his Quadricycle, which he drove in Detroit three months later, on June 4.

National Automotive History Collection, Detroit Public Library

Duryea drove a machine developed with his brother, Charles. Now, two years later, the Duryeas were about to give it more national visibility. While King had no entry, he wanted into the race. So he signed up as an umpire.

The weather that Thanksgiving morning was abysmal, the roads covered with 4 to 6 inches of snow, as well as 2-foot drifts in places, after a stormy day and night that had seen winds of up to 60 miles per hour. As a result the route was abbreviated – instead of from Chicago to Milwaukee, it would now be about 52 miles, from Jackson Park in Chicago to Evanston and return. Had the race not been postponed twice, leading the *Times-Herald* to the edge of ridicule, the organizers might well have delayed it.

But off they went – the Duryea, three imported Benz gasoline vehicles and two electrics. One of the Benz cars was called the Mueller-Benz because owner Hieronymus Mueller of Decatur, Ill., and his son Oscar had made alterations they felt justified the name. The electrics had no chance in the cold weather and retired early. Only two cars completed the race – the Duryea, driven by Frank, the winner in 10 hours and 23 minutes, finishing at 7:18 p.m., and the Mueller-Benz, which arrived 1 hour and 45 minutes later.

The Mueller-Benz finished only because King, who was umpire in the car, took the wheel when driver Oscar Mueller fainted late in the race. Mueller had been driving an open car in freezing weather for about nine hours with almost nothing to eat since breakfast. His passenger, Charles Reid, had fainted earlier and had been taken away by cutter. Under the rules, the starting driver had to be with the car at the end or it was disqualified. King drove to the finish, holding onto Mueller to keep him from falling out. Mueller went to the hospital (and recovered) and King went to the nearby Del Prado Hotel for "the most sumptuous Thanksgiving dinner" he ever had.

King was no doubt energized by the experience. Continuing his momentum, he advertised as a manufacturer of gasoline engines in Detroit late in 1895. On March 6, 1896, King drove a gasoline-fueled horseless carriage along Woodward Avenue in Detroit – credited as the first such drive in what would become the Motor City.

Gasoline engines: The obsession begins

The *Detroit Journal*, which remarked "the connecting rods fly like lightning," described King's vehicle as "a most unique machine," providing George May with a title for his 1975 book detailing Michigan auto history. A friend of King's followed him on a bicycle that night. His name was Henry Ford.

Ford, born in 1863 on a farm in what is now Dearborn, Mich., had a mechanical bent from childhood. In 1891, he took a position in Detroit with the Edison Illuminating Company, eventually becoming chief engineer. When Ford attended the 1893 fair in Chicago, he was particularly drawn to several gasoline engines. Ford began work on the engine for his first motor vehicle early in 1896 and was able to drive it in the early morning of June 4 that year. While King was first by three months, Ford's "Quadricycle" is seen as a more sophisticated work – a lightweight (500-pound) machine that could travel briskly at 25 miles per hour, a gazelle compared with King's ponderous 1,300-pound carriage that rumbled up Woodward at 5 to 8 mph.

Ransom Olds also benefited from the Chicago fair. He took advantage of an opportunity to ride in the Benz gasoline vehicle displayed there. Three years later, on August 11, 1896, only months after King and then Ford tested their first motor vehicles, Ransom Olds treated a newspaper reporter to a successful test ride in Lansing of his gasoline-powered vehicle.*

Meanwhile, back in Detroit, David Buick was becoming interested in gasoline engines and horseless carriages as well. He must have known something about what others were doing. King's drive had been reported, though sparingly, in the newspapers. Buick would likely have seen the stories. Information on advances in gasoline engines could also be found regularly in *Scientific American* and other magazines.

---

* While he trailed King and Ford by a few months, Olds had advantages in moving from a builder of one car to a manufacturer. Olds was already in charge of a booming manufacturing business in Lansing. Also, he and his company had been experimenting with engines, first steam and then gasoline, for more than a decade. In 1901, Olds, who was lured by financiers to build a factory in Detroit, produced about 425 curved-dash Oldsmobiles – becoming the first volume producer of automobiles in the United States even though a fire burned down his new plant in Detroit in March.

David Buick's Marvelous Motor Car

Known all Over the World

THE Buick Stationary Engine has been on the market for the past seven years, and is well known and fully guaranteed. We have a plant capable of turning out (2,600) twenty-six hundred engines per year. We want agents in every town. Write at once for agency.

BUICK MOTOR COMPANY
The Engine Builders   Flint, Mich.

Kevin Kirbitz
This 1904 ad in The Implement Age *appears to confirm Buick was marketing its engines in the late 19th century*

All that's recorded is what David Buick told his interviewer, Bruce Catton. And that was his recollection he became interested in gasoline engines in 1895. "I had one horse-drawn dray to take my goods to town, but I needed another. I couldn't afford a new team, although I got my second dray on credit; and I got to thinking about making an engine that would move the dray without horses."

Thinking about making an engine and becoming obsessed with engines was apparently a small step for David Buick. Certainly his passion for engines soon surpassed whatever interest he still had in plumbing inventions and supplies. But Buick's first forays into this field were not for automobiles. Buick was building and selling at least a few stationary and portable engines of an L-head design for farm use as early as 1897.

An L-head is a four-cycle engine with valves positioned in the block alongside the piston in roughly an L-shaped design. These engines could be set up for various farm work, such as churning milk, cutting feed or running a pump or a saw. It's likely Buick's engines were being hand-built at first, in very small numbers.*

---

* The four-cycle engine dates to 1877 when Nikolaus August Otto patented the "silent Otto" in Germany. The engine had four piston strokes per cycle. The first stroke sucked the fuel in, the second compressed it – with an explosion at the end of that stroke, the third or power stroke drove the piston back down, and

Gasoline engines: The obsession begins

Barn behind David Buick's house on Meldrum in Detroit, where some early engine and car work may have occurred.

A Buick Motor Company advertisement published in *The Implement Age* September 22, 1904, states "the Buick Stationary Engine has been on the market for the past seven years, and is well known and fully guaranteed." That ad, inferring Buick engine production began about 1897, is one of the few clues about Buick's engine activities in the 19th century. If true, it means David probably *was* beginning to work with engines by 1895 – quite early for a Detroiter.

However, Charles Hulse found an 1899 *Motor Vehicle Review* story saying David announced plans to enter the gasoline engine business that year. It's likely he had decided to take a step forward from building and selling a few engines as a sideline at Buick & Sherwood and get serious about creating a separate engine company. In the meantime, Buick & Sherwood was possibly finding some space for engine activity, although Buick and his elder son were also tinkering with engines in a barn behind their house.

---

the fourth exhausted the burned gases. This was an immediate sensation, an important advancement over the two-cycle, which combined the intake and compression functions into one stroke and the power and exhaust functions into a second.

William Sherwood in later years

Arthur Pound described Sherwood as having "an adventurous turn," and suggested he too was at least briefly involved in Buick & Sherwood's engine sideline. Maybe, but Sherwood could not have been totally pleased with Buick's new direction or work habits. "Dave, either get down to work or get out," he exploded finally, in the memory of a Sherwood granddaughter.

In 1899, the partners sold their plumbing business to the Standard Sanitary Manufacturing Company, headquartered in Pittsburgh, for $100,000. Buick had helped organize that firm and stayed with it for about a year. Sherwood eventually formed the Sherwood Brass Company (sold to Lear-Siegler in 1970).

Buick, with his new capital, began to ramp up his engine business. He hired a Canadian named W. S. Murray as his engine foreman (the year is unrecorded, but probably 1899). It is recorded that in 1899 Buick hired a Detroit machinist named Walter Lorenzo Marr as Murray's assistant.

Gasoline engines: The obsession begins

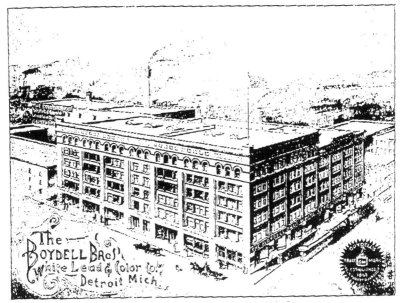

Boydell Building at Beaubien and Champlain (now Lafayette) in downtown Detroit, built late in the 19th century not long before this illustration was made, was still standing in the early 21st century. In 1900, Buick Auto-Vim and Power Company had space there, on the first or second floor at the corner.

The sale of the plumbing supply business was completed in December of 1899. Next Buick created a company – in late 1899 or early 1900 – with the vigorous name of Buick Auto-Vim and Power Company. Now he had a proper center for his engine experiments and production.

Buick Auto-Vim's address in the 1900 Detroit phone book is 139 Beaubien Street. Detroit addresses were revised in the early 1920s; in 1900, that address was at the southwest corner of Beaubien and Champlain (now Lafayette) in downtown Detroit. Buick Auto-Vim was on the first or second floor, at the corner, of the Boydell Building, a six-story red brick structure still standing more than a century later. There were numerous addresses within the large building (including Dodge Motor Works at about the same time). But 139 Beaubien was also used in 1900 by, among others, the Hygienic Seat Company, likely connected with Buick's previous line of work.

David Buick's Marvelous Motor Car

Buick sent Murray off to explore how to manufacture engines. A scrap of information survives suggesting Buick's plans and timing. On February 28, 1900, Murray showed up at the office of C.B. Calder, general superintendent of the Detroit Shipbuilding Company. In his diary, Calder noted Murray, whom he identified as an engineer for Buick & Sherwood, asked "if we could advise him in regard to the best mill for boring out gasoline engine cylinders (as) they are going in the business to make 20 engines a day." Recalled Calder: "We advised his going to the Westinghouse people."

(This is probably a reference to the Westinghouse Engine Company of Schenectady, N.Y., which incidentally hired Henry Ford in the early 1880s; for about a year Ford serviced the company's engines owned by farmers in southern Michigan.)

Twenty engines a day was an ambitious schedule. David Buick had clearly crossed the line, at least in his mind, from engine developer and tinkerer to serious manufacturer.

Chapter 4

Buick and boats

By early 1900, David Buick was aiming to broaden his reach. Branching out from making only stationary engines primarily for the farm, he listed the expertise of the new Buick Auto-Vim and Power Company in the 1900 Detroit phone book as "gas and gasoline engines & automobiles."

The company would also try motorizing boats. After all, David was a boating enthusiast – even if he did fancy sailboats. By 1898, he was vice commodore of the Detroit Yacht Club and was winning sailboat races with some regularity. That year he was a winner in his class in a big event, the Inter-Lakes Yachting Association (ILYA) Regatta, to this day held annually at Put-in-Bay, on South Bass Island in Lake Erie. He won with his 27-foot sailboat, the Carrie B., named for Caroline Buick. (A small brass cannon said to have been used by David as a regatta starting gun is still owned by a Buick great-grandson, Doug Boes.)

Almost nothing is known about Buick Auto-Vim's early engine manager, W.S. Murray, except he was hired for his expertise in marine engines. But Walter Marr is a different story. In 1899, Marr was 34 and newly employed by the Detroit Shipbuilding Company after selling a bicycle shop. Eight weeks into the job, he was working with friends on a powerboat motor when Buick, walking along the dock, observed him with great interest. Buick's attraction to boats and his new work in gasoline engines were no doubt coming together in his mind. David was ready to build marine engines, and Marr must have looked like someone who could help that idea along. Buick immediately hired Marr as Murray's assistant.

In the spring of 1900, Murray struggled at Buick Auto-Vim to build an engine and install it in a boat. Murray was having problems

David Buick's Marvelous Motor Car

The young Walter Lorenzo Marr.

and Marr did him no favors. Marr recalled: "I knew it (the engine) was wrong but he was my boss and during the daytime I had to take his order... But at night I would take the engine down and build it up again according to my notions. I always had it back the way he built it by the next morning."

Murray was stumped in designing an "elbow" in the drive train to carry power from the engine to the propeller. The elbow had too great an angle, Marr remembered, and "it nearly knocked the bottom out of the boat when we tried to run it." Buick became impatient with Murray and turned to Marr.

"Marr, can you put that motor in there the way it should go?" Buick asked.

Marr did. "All right, Marr," said Buick. "You're the new boss."

According to Marr, Murray was eventually fired over this. It must

A few years later, Marr as Buick chief engineer.

have been early in the year, because the Detroit City Directory for 1900 lists David Buick as president of Buick Auto-Vim and Power Company and Walter Marr as manager, engines.

Recalling the boat in a luncheon club speech decades later, Marr related: "I built it the way I wanted to and the ship beat any boat on the river" in its class.

This was probably the 20-foot boat Buick sold to one Albert Stegmeyer, who in 1899-1901 turned his bathhouse on the Detroit River into a gasoline launch livery. In November 1901, Stegmeyer wrote to David, praising the Buick engine in that launch. The letter mentioned he had bought the boat and motor from the Buick company two years earlier, seemingly dating it to 1899. More likely, work on this first documented Buick marine engine was begun in 1899 and was completed in spring 1900. Stegmeyer probably counted the 1900

David Buick's Marvelous Motor Car

and 1901 boating seasons as two years.

As for the engine itself, Stegmeyer praised it as "the best there is on the Detroit River…I can beat every one except a 30-foot launch which has a 12 H.P. engine against my 3 H.P., but it does not beat me very much…." He compared the Buick engine to others in his livery. "Whenever you go down to the livery you will see several owners of the different boats fixing up their engines, and it seems there is always something the matter with them…I have had absolutely no trouble at all with my engine…."

David was so pleased with Stegmeyer's endorsement he had the letter printed in his first three engine catalogs.

Chapter 5

First Buick automobile

While Buick Auto-Vim and Power Company worked to perfect marine engines for its product line, Walter Marr also focused on the automobile – this was why he had come to Detroit in the first place. Marr, the company's new engine manager, was no doubt encouraged by David Buick – both were enchanted with the horseless carriage.

They were similar in other ways. Like David, Marr was small in stature, about 120 pounds, and at 5-foot-6 a half-inch taller than Buick. Like David, Marr lost his father when he was very young. George Ernest Marr died when Walter was 6, leaving the family with no money. Like David, Marr loved to work with mechanical devices, always looking for ways to make them better and simpler. And also like David, Marr could be quick to anger, and in general was a difficult person to work with.

Still, for Buick, Marr seemed a good catch. Since David had made automobiles a stated element of Buick Auto-Vim's purpose, Marr set out to build one. It would not be his first.

Marr was born August 14, 1865, in Lexington, a small town on the shore of Lake Huron in Michigan's Thumb. Late in the decade the family moved to East Tawas, across Saginaw Bay and up the Lake Huron shore. After his father died, a local man, Sam Anker, took an interest in him and persuaded John Walker, owner of an engineering firm, to hire him in 1882 as an apprentice. Marr was 17 and this was the beginning of his career as a machinist.

Moving in 1888 to Saginaw, a much larger city south of East Tawas, Marr went to work for Wicks Brothers, a company of sawmill and steamboat engineers. There he built his first gas engine, a motor designed by his superintendent. Marr experimented with a variety of carburetors and other devices on that engine. Later that year, when he

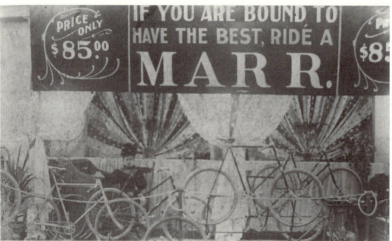

Walter Marr and his bicycle shop at Grand River and Second in Detroit, where Marr built his first automobile. Henry Ford was said to have had a shop nearby.

First Buick automobile

opened a shop to make and repair bicycles in Saginaw, he learned to use other engines – a Hercules, a Philadelphia Otto and a Sintz – in the manufacturing process.

The bicycle business was booming in this period, so Marr was cashing in on the latest craze. But always, he had his eye on the automobile. "I liked the idea of a horseless carriage from the minute I heard about it up in Saginaw," he told a *Detroit News* reporter in 1939. "So I moved my business into Detroit, opening a bicycle shop at Grand River and Second and began experimenting with gasoline engines." He made the move in 1896.

If he wanted to build automobiles, Marr could hardly have chosen a better time or place to set up his bicycle shop than in 1896 at Grand River and Second avenues in Detroit. This was only several blocks from 58 Bagley Avenue, where Henry Ford built his first automobile, the Quadricycle, that year in a little workshop behind the house. It would be interesting to know exactly when in that year Marr arrived, because in the middle of a rainy night on June 4, 1896, Ford – after famously knocking bricks out of the doorway of his tiny workshop so he could get his machine out the door – motored down Grand River, driving his first automobile for the first time.

As noted, Ford was a friend of Charles B. King, who a few months before had driven the first gasoline-powered automobile in Detroit. There seems to have been a good deal of sharing of information and even hardware among those two and perhaps other early Detroit automobile enthusiasts, such as Barton Peck, who came from a wealthy family, and Charles G. Annesley, about whom more will be said later. Both were reportedly building or trying to build motor vehicles.

How much Marr knew about Ford and his automobile experiments is unclear. He once said that when he first talked to Ford, to his knowledge Ford had not yet built a motor vehicle. That's possible, but most likely he had. Ford shared information only when it suited him. One of his close friends said he did not know until years later that Ford was building motor cars.

But Marr did talk often about his conversations with Ford. And it's hard to believe that if they talked about cars, and Marr's shop

David Buick's Marvelous Motor Car

Walter Marr (right) and employee Will Staring with Marr's first automobile, the 'motor wagon' with four-cylinder motor, probably in Marr's Detroit bike shop. Marr said he 'perfected' this vehicle in 1898. This was before Marr built his first Buick automobile.

in 1896 was so close to Ford's Bagley Avenue shop, that he wasn't aware of Ford's activities. Even if Ford were being secretive, there must have been echoes up and down Grand River about Ford's successful drive of his Quadricycle in the summer of 1896.

Marr continued to use small engines in his bicycle-making busi-

First Buick automobile

ness, adding a 6.5-horsepower Olds and a 7-horsepower Cofield to drive the machinery in his Detroit shop. He soon began to meet horseless carriage enthusiasts such as Annesley and Peck. Bicycle shops were great places to work on horseless carriages – with precision tools, power equipment and finely built components such as wheels, gears, sprockets and chains at hand.

At some point, Marr decided to build what he called a "motor wagon," working in his shop. He didn't say when he started, but boasted he perfected it in 1898. His first motorized vehicle looks in a photo as if it were created from bicycle wheels, a frame and a carriage body. It was powered by a four-cylinder, four-cycle engine.

Using four cylinders was unusual at that time, and would seem especially so for a man building, in a bicycle shop, his first horseless carriage. Bill Close, husband of Marr's granddaughter Sarah, offers an intriguing theory.

When King first drove his horseless carriage in Detroit in March of 1896, he used a four-cylinder engine he had created himself. Close suggests that very engine or, more specifically, the engine block, may have been used by Marr in his first motor wagon. Close labels his theory as "sheer speculation" but it sounds possible.

George May, quoting Oliver Barthel, who was King's assistant at the time King made his first Detroit drive, said "a freeze-up" cracked King's engine block later in March of 1896 and he sold the engine together with blueprints and patterns to Charles Annesley. And Annesley became so well acquainted with Marr that he was, within a year or so, building an automobile in Marr's bicycle shop. Close speculates Annesley could have sold or loaned the engine or engine block to Marr, who used it as the basis on which to build his own engine, which he installed in his first motor wagon. We'll come back to this theory. Marr once said he built the car for $1.50, which sounds like a vehicle built from old bicycle wheels and borrowed engine components. Eventually he sold it for $300.

Whatever the source of Marr's engine, he had a lot of trouble with it at first. "When you took it out it would start on four cylinders and you would get home on one; then you'd take the head off and pick out the pieces," he said.

Most of the weight – the engine and water tank – was in the rear. And so, he remembered, the car would sometimes rear up like a "bucking bronco" when he started it. He would be driving in "starts and jerks" while bystanders stood along the road "laughing their heads off." One shouted derisively, "Why don't you get a horse? Who would want a thing like that?"

According to Marr, one bystander didn't laugh. Henry Ford just watched Marr's car and then talked to him about it.

Marr blamed the engine's hot-tube ignition for the trouble. Removing that primitive system, he said he smoothed the performance by fitting the engine with an electrical ignition and a spark advance, or what an interviewer called "novel electric ignition features, arranged to advance the time of the hammer spark production." By changing the point in the piston's travel within the cylinder where the spark was introduced, he made the engine run more smoothly. In an interview with Charles Hulse in 1934, Marr claimed this was the first use of a spark advance in the country.

Another interviewer reported: "Ford, who had a shop across the corner from Mr. Marr's, saw his car come up the street and make a smooth stop, which was unusual. The next morning Ford was waiting to see Mr. Marr and ask him what he had done to his car."

Compared with Henry Ford, Marr was obviously playing catch-up in his knowledge of automobiles. By 1898, when Marr said he perfected his four-cylinder car, Ford's Quadricycle was already nearly two years behind him and Ford was at work on his second automobile. Ford and his wife Clara had moved from Bagley Avenue in June of 1897. But Ford may well have been in position to talk to Marr. As Sidney Olson wrote in his excellent book, *Young Henry Ford,* Ford's life from 1898 to mid 1902 "is the despair of biographers" because it is hard to track his activities. "In this period Henry is a real slippery creature...he slides along for a month or two and then pops up in a dozen places at once." And as David L. Lewis, author of *The Public Image of Henry Ford,* told the writer, Ford and Marr had some things in common. Both had a mechanical bent, both lost their father during

Walter Marr, joined by wife Abbie, drives the first Buick automobile, built in the 1899-1901 time frame, on a Detroit street. Marr built the car, which had a one-cylinder engine, and later bought it from David Buick.

childhood, each moved to Detroit to seek his fortune, and both was fond of bicycles.

Marr once commented that when he built his first automobile, it was one of only three in Detroit. If true, King must have been between cars, because Marr listed the other two automobile owners as Henry Ford and Barton Peck. Peck no doubt got special attention from Ford because Peck's father was president of Edison Illuminating, where Ford was chief engineer.

There's little to suggest David Buick was interacting with this group of Detroit automobile and gas engine enthusiasts, outside of the possibility Buick and Ford knew each other from their differ-

On March 25, 1901, David Buick asks Walter Marr to resign.

ent periods of apprenticeship at James Flower & Brothers. Certainly Marr – soon to be Buick's most important employee – was talking to Ford, Annesley, Peck and probably King and others. Marr was likely Buick's best link to Detroit's earliest "car guys."

Marr said his bicycle business was successful until a partner ruined it. The unnamed partner gets the blame, but the bicycle craze was ending abruptly about this time and a lot of bike shops were going away. While never discussing the details of his firm's business disaster, Marr made it clear he was devastated. "I was all right with people until a partner ruined my bicycle factory," he said in the 1930s. "Then I didn't trust anybody. Ruined in the bicycle business, with no money and no credit after the failure, I remembered what my first friend (perhaps a reference to Sam Anker back in East Tawas) had said about learning a trade and sticking to it. I wanted to build a machine."

Marr built a motor-driven tricycle in 1899, figuring if he could demonstrate he was a good machinist, he could always get a job. This two-passenger vehicle, he said, "ran to the complete satisfaction of its purchaser." The 118-pound tricycle, according to Marr, was also important because of the configuration of its engine, which will be explained later.

Marr's talents as an inventor and machinist gave him the ability to see a process, borrow it and improve it, as demonstrated several times in his career. In the bicycle business, he heard a nearby factory had an improved process of turning out sprockets. He said he made 14 trips to that factory, trying to slip into the part of the shop where the sprockets were manufactured. Finally he saw the process and was able to copy it – and then improve it. Another quality was his determination to improve his work. He once commented that while other men were at lunch, "I was whittling at some better tool or machine." Bitter about his various setbacks in business, Marr told his brother: "Every dog has his day. I ain't had mine yet, but I will."

After closing his bicycle shop, working at Detroit Shipbuilding and then arriving at Buick Auto-Vim, Marr built his third motor vehicle as part of his job. It was the first automobile to be called a Buick. Pioneer auto reporter Hugh Dolnar, discussing its development in *Cycle and Automobile Trade Journal* in 1903, said Marr built the vehicle in 1900.

Dolnar reported the first Buick car was driven by a single-cylinder, 4-inch bore by 5-inch stroke, horizontal, water-cooled engine with jump spark ignition. This vehicle "had a chain transmission, and in the motor Marr was the first of a group of Detroit experimenters in automobile origination to use the jump spark."[*]

---

[*] Jump-spark ignition is the use of high voltage to jump a spark across a gap and ignite the fuel and air charge inside the cylinder. It was a major advance over the old hot-tube ignition, which was simply a tube inside the cylinder that was heated red hot by a candle or alcohol burner or some other external heat source. The red hot tube would start the combustion process within the cylinder. Ransom Olds

David Buick's Marvelous Motor Car

Marr later added detail: The car had a three-point suspension, underslung springs and 44-inch buggy wheels. He confirmed a surviving photograph of Marr and his wife Abbie in a buggy-wheeled automobile was of this car and was taken in Detroit – a photo of the first experimental Buick (contradicting published reports the photo was taken in Cleveland, Ohio).

Bill Close, husband of Marr's granddaughter, Sarah, said this first Buick's engine probably came right off the shelf of Buick Auto-Vim and Power Company. It may well have been designed by Marr, as the firm's engines manager, or even by David Buick. Marr was enthusiastic about his new car. He reminisced: "I remember that when I finished the first automobile that ever bore the name of Buick, I tried it out on the only proving grounds we had – Cass Avenue just north of Grand River. What a day that was!"

There's proof the first Buick automobile existed in 1901. But there are also reports it was built in 1896, 1898 and 1899 as well as 1900, with the information usually traced to Marr. By the 1930s, Marr had settled on 1898…or maybe '99. And even Dolnar contradicted himself, once reporting Marr and Buick built the first Buick automobile in 1896 after earlier writing Marr had built it in 1900. Conflicting news articles abound in this period. The opinion here is Marr may have started building his first automobile for Buick by 1899 but likely did most of the work in 1900.

Most of the debate regarding dates undoubtedly stems from con-

---

applied for a patent on his gasoline vehicle on September 18, 1896, that went beyond hot tube to an electric igniter. An electric igniter could be connected to a battery or other power source and would glow red hot, thus igniting the fuel and air charge. When a question arose of whether a car could have a spark advance (the four-cylinder car) without a jump spark, GM engineer Kevin Kirbitz advised one form of early electrical ignition produced a low-tension spark and therefore "a spark advance would be theoretically possible even without jump-spark ignition." Indeed, the Buick Manufacturing Company catalog of 1902 or 1903 mentions both types. It says "we use the jump spark and not the mechanical spark, the former being much more simple and not so liable to get out of order and give trouble." So technically Marr's first car could have had the first spark advance and the second car (the first Buick) the first jump spark among the Detroit automobiles, as Dolnar wrote.

First Buick automobile

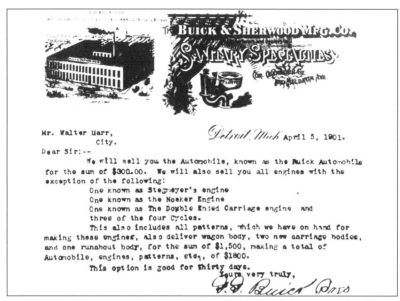

On April 5, 1901, David Buick offers to sell the 'Buick-Automobile' to Walter Marr, along with engines and carriage bodies – the earliest known written reference to a Buick car.

On August 16, 1901, the first Buick automobile is sold to Walter Marr at a 'discount' – $225 instead of David Buick's earlier asking price of $300.

fusion about which vehicle Marr or the writer is referring to – his first motor wagon, with four cylinders, or his first Buick automobile, with one cylinder. In talking to newspaper reporters, he may not have felt it mattered to differentiate between the two for the purpose of whatever point he was making. And probably the reporters – and auto historians – sometimes got things mixed up.

Anxious for David Buick to see the new Buick car, Marr said he was able to entice his boss to visit his shop only once. Buick and Marr "went for a ride in the Buick car," a reporter wrote in covering a Marr speech in 1934. "The vibrator stuck, stalling the car. Buick was disgusted. A street car was passing and he boarded it."

Marr was furious at the snub. He immediately offered to quit. David Buick, equally mercurial, accepted. Marr kept this letter from David, dated March 25, 1901: "After considering the conversation that we had the other day, and wherein you offered your resignation, I have concluded it is best for both parties to accept the same, and to take effect at once. You will please turn over the keys, and such other articles that you may have to Mr. Sherwood, and oblige."

Buick's note was on old Buick & Sherwood letterhead, the style decorated with a drawing of that firm's most celebrated product – a toilet. Using up that stationery could hardly have left the impression Buick Auto-Vim was an up-and-coming business. (Another clue: No one ever found any Buick Auto-Vim literature or ads beyond the one-liner in the 1900 Detroit phone book and repeated in the city directory). The letter also reveals William Sherwood was still around, at least in control of the shop premises.

One possible reason for David's 1901 split with Marr, other than an angry exchange of words, was money – Buick may have been running out of it. On April 5, 1901, less than two weeks after their split, David offered to sell Marr the Buick automobile (the one Marr built while employed by Buick) as well as engines and carriage bodies.

This is the earliest known written reference to a Buick automobile: "We will sell you the Automobile, known as the Buick Automobile for the sum of $300.00," Buick wrote to Marr. He also offered Marr "all engines" with a few exceptions, and included in the offer all patterns for making them, as well as a delivery body, two new carriage bodies and one runabout body for an additional $1,500. The exceptions were "One known as Stegmeyer's engine, One known as the Noeker Engine, One known as The Double Ended Carriage engine and three of the four cycles."

Students of Buick history make much of this letter. Not only was it the earliest mention of a Buick automobile, it also hinted at the company's other work. With an inventory of carriages and engines, the Buick firm was probably contemplating, if not already working on, another automobile besides the one developed by Marr.

The Stegmeyer and Noeker engines excluded from the offering in Buick's letter were likely being worked on for those customers. Stegmeyer's was probably a marine engine. The Noeker may have been for use at Joseph Noeker's printing company.

There was no quick response to the letter. Marr, needing a job in a hurry after departing Buick, hired in with the new Oldsmobile plant in Detroit that was being rebuilt after a disastrous fire in March. Marr said he built three of the first curved-dash Oldsmobiles completed as production resumed.

At Olds, he found himself in a situation reminiscent of the one with W.S. Murray and the Buick marine engine. As Marr himself related, the first Oldsmobile he worked on had a problem – it ran fine when the car was turned to the left but the engine stopped when it was turned right. He and his foreman tore the car down 35 times. Finally the foreman asked Marr: "What do you think the trouble is?"

Marr responded: "You ought to put a few more staples in the wire." They did, and it worked.

"How long have you known that?" the foreman asked.

"Since the second time we tore it down," Marr replied.

When asked why he hadn't told his boss, Marr replied he hadn't been asked and was hired to do as he was told. When his employer heard of the incident, according to Marr, he fired the foreman and gave Marr the job.

But he wasn't there long. He left on a Saturday night because he had heard there would be a strike the following Monday, and he didn't believe in strikes. (The strike began in late May of 1901). He was out of work six weeks – a rarity for him – and then perfected a bicycle motor for the Detroit Brass, Iron and Novelty Company in a short assignment.

Finally, there was a breakthrough regarding Buick's letter. In August of 1901, Marr traveled to Cleveland, Ohio, following a job opportunity. He said he gave his wife all his money except a dollar and told her he was going to Cleveland to build automobiles "and won't be back until I do." He used the dollar for boat ferry to Cleveland and skipped breakfast because he was then broke. But he was hired shortly after arriving in Cleveland by the American Motor Carriage Company and given $6 in advance pay.

He then returned to Detroit and took up Buick on his April offer. On August 16, 1901, he bought the "Buick Automobile" from Buick – but for $225, not $300. The first Buick car was sold at a discount. He was able to buy it because the purchase price came from the Cleveland firm. Marr took the car to Cleveland as part of Marr's contract to build automobiles for American Motor Carriage. The first Buick car would become the pilot for this company's new automobile.

Meanwhile, late in 1901 or more likely 1902, Buick Auto-Vim and Power Company was reconstituted as Buick Manufacturing Company, headquartered at 416-418 Howard Street (now 10-12 Howard) near Twelfth Street in Detroit. Although it still made several types of engines, David Buick would begin to concentrate on something new.

Somehow, he had discovered a new engine design, with the valves positioned at the top of the combustion chamber. It seemed to have some definite advantages. This overhead-valve design didn't have a name yet, but the company would come up with its own label. For much of the 20th century, Buick would be famous for its "valve-in-head" engines.

Chapter 6

Charles Annesley: Finding a missing link

In March of 1901, months before his connection with the American Motor Carriage Company, Walter Marr wrote to an old friend. Marr was then in need of a job after his departure from Buick Auto-Vim and Power Company.

Charles George Annesley, then an executive at the Buffalo (New York) Gasolene Motor Company, replied on March 28, 1901. He told Marr he was "awfully surprised to hear that you had left the Buick concern, as I thought that you were getting along nicely." Annesley said his firm had no openings, but might later. He advised Marr: "My boy, shake the dust of a slow old Detroit off your feet, and go east with some good responsible house where your abilities will be appreciated."

And Annesley added what became a classic paragraph: "What is poor old Ford doing? I feel so sorry for him. He is a good man and perfectly capable, and yet cannot get out of the hole just because he won't leave Detroit."

The letter is also remarkable because it is between the first buyer of a Ford (Annesley, purchaser of Henry Ford's Quadricycle), and the soon-to-be first buyer of a Buick (Marr).

Beyond that, it's fair to ask who is Charles Annesley and why is he important?

Answering the second question first, Annesley is important – or, more accurately, interesting in auto history – because he was one of the very few persons known to have worked in the industry's earliest years, in the late 19th century, with men who helped form the beginning of the two giant U.S. automakers – Ford and General Motors. Annesley was an associate of both Walter Marr (whose abilities helped make Buick a success and therefore led to the creation of GM)

David Buick's Marvelous Motor Car

```
                                PHILIP DOHN, Vice-Pres.                    A. SNYDER, Sec'y and Treas.

                                Buffalo Gasolene Motor Co.,
                                        Cor. Dewitt and Bradley Streets.
                                     MANUFACTURERS OF
                                     ...Motors...
                                     For Vehicle and Marine Purposes.
                                Telephone Amherst 103.
                                Cable Address "Fischer."
                                                    BUFFALO, N. Y.,    Mar. 28th       1901

My dear Walter:-
        I was awfully surprised to hear that you had left the Buick
concern, as I thought that you were getting along so nicely.
        We are turning out eight complete engines a week and have put
in $5000.00 worth of the latest machinery, we have shipped 24  engines
to England, and almost all of our U.S. business is for salt water.
        We are going to put up a line of launches, and have two of
our own this summer.
        We have all the help we require at present, but perhaps we will
put a good hustling salesman on the road a little later on.
        My boy shake the dust of slow old Detroit off your feet, and
go east with some good responsible house where your abilities will
be appreciated.
        What the Devil do you think would have become of me if I had
stayed there.  Here I have the very nicest of a  Company, good salary,
and Stock in the concern.
        What is poor old Ford doing?  I feel so very sorry for him
he is a good man and perfectly capable, and yet cannot get out of the
hole just because he won't leave Detroit.
        Peck tells me that he got turned down by that puke Whitcombe
another sample of what they do in Detroit.  Write me soon
                        Sincerely
                            Chas.G.Annesley
```

Famous letter from Charles G. Annesley (first buyer of a Ford car) to Walter Marr (first buyer of a Buick car) asking, 'What is poor old Ford doing?'

and Henry Ford. He was also a friend of Charles B. King, the man who was first to drive a gasoline car in Detroit.

Not only did Annesley buy Henry Ford's first car, he also bought the freeze-cracked engine from Charles B. King's first car – the one

Charles Annesley: Finding a missing link

that made that historical drive in downtown Detroit. And if Marr's relative, Bill Close, is correct, Annesley may have provided the engine or engine block to Marr for his first motor car – pre-Buick.

An article in the September 4, 1899, *Detroit Tribune* provides solid evidence of the Annesley-Marr relationship and also suggests Marr's bicycle store was becoming a shop of choice for building horseless carriages.

> C. G. Annesley…is building a machine at the establishment of Walter L. Marr on Second avenue, near Grand River. Mr. Annesley has an engine of his own design, a four-cylindered reciprocating motioned affair that is not more than one-sixth the size of a horse and pulls like a 12-ox team. Mr. Annesley has built, when this one is done, six automobiles, and no two alike. Each one was built to order practically. This last one is being prepared for service on heavy sandy roads north of Chicago to Cook county. It will be ready in about two weeks and will be given a speed trial here before it is shipped away.

The article also talks about Walter Marr's motor tricycle:

> Mr. Marr is himself…building a tricycle to be run by a gasoline motor of his own design. His motor is a great source of pride to him and excites general admiration on account of its very small size. He designed it himself, and it sits most inconspicuously in its bracket under the seat on the tricycle. This machine will soon be put out on the road also.

Despite what should have been Annesley's highly visible position in automotive history, he was virtually unknown for many years. George May described Annesley as a "shadowy figure who is best remembered as the man who bought Henry Ford's first car."

The biggest reason Annesley was a "shadowy figure" – or worse, completely unknown – is because his name was misspelled as "Ainsley" in Henry Ford's first book, *My Life and Work,* published in 1922. Ford wrote he sold his first automobile, the Quadricycle, "to Charles Ainsley of Detroit for two hundred dollars." Surprisingly, virtually every auto historian since then picked up the misspelled name and never corrected it.

Finally, two historians figured it out. Sidney Olson in *Young Henry Ford* (1963) spelled the last name correctly. George May in *A Most Unique Machine* (1975) was first to note Annesley had been misspelled as Ainsley all those years.

As Michael W. R. Davis, a journalist, automotive historian and retired Ford public relations executive, once commented: "Because Ford's memory was faulty, he couldn't spell or (his 1922 collaborator Samuel) Crowther was an indifferent researcher, the name of the first purchaser of a Ford-built car went down mis-identified and largely lost from history."

Davis, who took a history course from George May at Eastern Michigan University, decided to further clean up the record by making Annesley the subject of his master's thesis in 1982. It was never published, and Davis had to hunt for a copy among his papers when he learned this writer was working on an account of David Buick's career, which in an oblique way includes Annesley.

The basic connection is that Buick's first chief engineer, Walter Marr, worked closely with Annesley on engines for a period and may have benefited from Annesley's relationship with Henry Ford and Charles B. King. Whatever Marr learned from Annesley, Ford and King, he likely carried over with him to the Buick organization. David Buick and his associates, therefore, were not working totally independent of the other Detroit auto pioneers – which might have been assumed but was never as fully documented.

Unmasking the mystery man, Davis learned Annesley had been born in Bundelkund, India, March 13, 1863, to an Irish mother and English father. He died of a heart attack in Providence Hospital, Detroit, June 10, 1925. His occupation was listed as electrical salesman. His wife, Charlotte Minchener of Detroit, had died two years earlier.

Davis wrote that "Sadly, at the time *My Life and Work* was published, Ford's first customer, Charles G. Annesley, was living (and was soon to die) in obscurity only a few blocks from Henry's office at the Highland Park Plant, home of the Model T."

Charles Annesley: Finding a missing link

Charles G. Annesley

Looking back at Annesley's career, George May quoted sources as stating Annesley and Barton Peck "each had their cars running before Henry Ford had his out" but they were poorly built and "did not last long." Annesley also took the King engine, which he had acquired from King together with the patterns and blueprints, and, according to May, "formed the Buffalo Gas Engine Company. The design was used by this company and made in different sizes for marine use."

Bill Close speculates Marr improved the engine Annesley received from King by adding the spark advance for his first motor wagon, then returned it to Annesley. In one interview, Marr said he sold the patent for a spark advance to the Buffalo firm. Close believes Marr actually sold the engine with the spark advance to Annesley, who then patented it on behalf of the Buffalo Gasolene Motor Company. Close has some of the evidence – he owns an early engine from the Buffalo company, and the patent number traces to Annesley.

Davis finally tracked down a nephew of Annesley who remembered him in his mid 50s as "rather bald, but a cheerful, very well-knit little man, about 5-foot-6 and very muscular. My recollection is that he was a broad jumper and a runner – he established a broad jump record that stood for many years at the Detroit Athletic Club."

The nephew remembered Annesley made a living selling electrical components to contractors, and that he was "of such talent mechanically that nothing was ever broken beyond repair around the house." About 1923, Henry Ford contacted Annesley and offered him a job. But he sent him off to see his aide Harry Bennett, who wanted him to start as an hourly employee in the engine plant. "And as far as Charlie was concerned, the hell with that noise," the nephew remembered.

Davis could find no record of what had happened to Annesley at the Buffalo Gasolene Motor Company, or what happened to the numerous automobiles Annesley was said to have built. Davis was able, however, to document Annesley's eventual return to Detroit, the city he had disparaged in his 1901 letter to Marr. But after his move to Buffalo, Charles Annesley – with the exception of one fascinating letter – vanishes from the story of Walter Marr and David Buick. His role had been a small one, an automobile enthusiast who had worked with both Henry Ford and Marr, Buick's first chief engineer, but it deserved to be remembered.

Chapter 7

'Valve-in-head' engines

Overhead valve. "Valve-in-head." Whatever you called it, this advance in gasoline engine design quickly became the big story in Buick's operations. It was a "rare mechanical idea," in the words of an early Buick catalog. Buick can't claim it conceived the idea – or was even the first to use it in an American automobile. But it can claim it was the first manufacturer to get it right – to successfully integrate all of the key elements of the modern overhead-valve engine. Buick was also likely the first to fully understand the significance of the design – and certainly it was the first to fully promote it.

With the valves positioned at the top of the combustion chamber, instead of in the block like most other engines of the time, the Buick design was more efficient than engines with other valve configurations. It was powerful and reliable, and eventually the entire industry would make use of the principle.

To Terry Dunham, writing in *Antique Automobile* in 1995, "the overhead-valve engine was the single most important mechanical factor in the early success of the Buick car. In fact, the ohv engine was one of the most important automobile advances ever."

The Buick people didn't fully understand its importance at first. When Buick began building overhead-valve stationary engines, the company emphasized "ease of manufacture and ease of service" as primary advantages.

The real benefit – the ability of the overhead-valve engine to breathe better and thus produce more horsepower per cubic inch of displacement than other engines – was discovered later. Walter Marr explained it this way to a reporter: Compression in a valve-in-head motor bears directly on the pistons, without any loss in jumping from valve chamber to valve chamber. "It's from 20 to 25 percent more powerful and efficient in performance (compared with other engines)," he told Sam Adkins of the *Chattanooga Free Press* in 1936.

As early as 1917, Buick Motor Company explained it another way. The company advertised that its engine's "small, simple, compact combustion chamber with the smallest possible water-jacketed space" gave it a "more perfect combustion than other types of motors, a quicker ignition of the charge and a smaller loss of heat through the water jackets. The sum of these advantages is more power and less gasoline consumption."

The engine was a key to the early success of Buick automobiles. As Billy Durant, who would save Buick and found General Motors, wrote in the 1930s: "With Buick we sold the assurance that the power to perform was there. Power sold Buick and made it what it is today." The first sentence in that quotation may be as important as the second. Once Durant, that master salesman, understood the significance of the engine, he promoted it heavily. The buying public was soon well aware "the power to perform was there."

In Buick Motor Company's early days, David Buick was publicized as the company's engine expert. The 1905 Buick automobile catalog refers vaguely to "a rare mechanical idea which found its first inception in the marine engine designed by Mr. D.D. Buick, an engine since adapted to and perfected in an automobile." The catalog says the engine's development of "phenomenal power in relation to size and weight of vehicle has never been approached by any competitor in the field."

But the catalog (probably written under Durant's direct supervision if not by the man himself) says David disclaimed credit for the automobile as a whole. That's because the car "embodies many distinctive features, some of which have been contributed by other men of inventive genius...notably, Mr. Walter L. Marr, who was distinctly a pioneer in this field, having personally built two of the first gasoline engines ever designed in this country. The Buick automobile is, therefore, a composite creature, embodying the results of long years of earnest thought and exhaustive tests...."

David Buick is giving Marr generous credit, but not for the en-

'Valve-in-head' engines

gine and its "rare mechanical idea," which is generally interpreted to mean the overhead-valve design.

Even Durant, who became a close friend of Marr, described David Buick as "a gas engine expert … very largely responsible for the creation of the marvelous motor which bears his name." Durant's daughter Margery said her father kept the Buick name on the automobile Durant promoted because he wanted to honor "the man who invented the engine." Once, she said, she and her father and David Buick sat in a shed while David described the workings of the engine.

Occasionally early employees sent their written memories to the company. Frank J. DeLaney documented his 1903-06 employment at Buick with a letter purportedly from David Buick. In a two-page remembrance, DeLaney said, "Mr. Dave Buick conceived the idea of building a stationary single cylinder valve-in-head motor…completed in the early spring of 1903." He credited Marr with later building the two-cylinder valve-in-head engine, which DeLaney said he assembled and tested under Marr's direction. But DeLaney was no doubt unaware of the company's documented work with overhead-valve engines dating to 1901 and also that other sources do not credit Marr for Buick's first two-cylinder overhead-valve engine.

The basic overhead-valve design was developed in Europe. When it came to the United States, Buick was not quite the first to use it in an automobile. It may have shown up first in an automobile in Syracuse, N.Y., where engineer John Wilkinson built an air-cooled, four-cylinder, overhead-valve engine for his experimental car in 1898. His attempt to produce his own car quickly failed. But he soon linked up with Herbert H. Franklin, who headed the H.H. Franklin Manufacturing Company – a Syracuse firm that is said to have invented the term "die casting." In 1902 Franklin and Wilkinson produced the first 219 Franklins. They had engines similar to Wilkinson's original – air cooled, four cylinders, overhead valves (see related article by Kevin Kirbitz at the end of this chapter). The Franklin automobile did well for many years but production ended in 1934 during the Great Depression. Franklin engines were produced for many more years, however, powering helicopters, aircraft and the Tucker Torpedo.

65

David Buick's Marvelous Motor Car

Also, Howard Marmon built an experimental car with an air-cooled engine using overhead valves in Indianapolis, Ind., in 1901 or 1902 and began production with 25 cars in 1905. Marmon abandoned air cooling in 1909. In 1911 Ray Harroun won the first Indianapolis 500 in his Marmon Wasp – but since Marmon left overhead valves from 1909 to 1915, the winning Wasp had a T-head motor. Marmon production ended in 1933, another victim of the Depression – which Buick barely survived.

How the overhead-valve design came to Buick is debated. But the paper trail favors Eugene C. Richard, an engineer who arrived in the United States from France in 1888. Richard was born April 8, 1867, in Savoy, and apprenticed with an uncle in a machine shop before moving to the United States. He then worked in Rochester, N.Y., and in Philadelphia.

In 1898, he moved his family to Detroit but jobs there were hard to find. According to Charles Hulse, who relates details apparently gathered from Richard's close relatives and not found elsewhere, Richard finally caught on as a machinist in Lansing, Mich., at the Kneeland Crystal Creamery, where he worked for two years. While there he designed and invented a cream separator and also helped a local dentist develop a mechanical device for drilling teeth. In the fall of 1900 he returned to Detroit to be with his family and got a job as a machinist at the newly built factory of Olds Motor Works, in the gasoline stationary and marine engine department.

A coincidence changed his career. As previously mentioned, a fire destroyed the Olds plant on March 9, 1901, temporarily stopping production of the Oldsmobile, the first mass-produced U.S. car. As a result, Richard was out of a job. Later that month, Walter Marr, after his rift with David Buick, left Buick Auto-Vim and Power Company. David eventually placed a want ad in the *Detroit News* for a skilled machinist and draftsman, and in May Richard responded and was hired. Choosing Richard to develop his engines was another case of great recruiting by David Buick. Richard (who pronounced it RICH-ard, not ri-SHARD, despite his French heritage) was not only less argumentative than Marr, he was also a knowledgeable and inventive engineer.

'Valve-in-head' engines

Eugene C. Richard, who may have brought overhead-valve engine design to Buick, with his wife Louisa

Richard provided a rare peek into Buick Auto-Vim. He said he was designer, draftsman, factory superintendent and foreman of a force of about six persons including the watchman and elevator boy, a newspaper reported. Shortly after his arrival, Richard increased the horsepower of Buick marine engines from two to five – considered a big achievement, although it involved only a slight changing of the timing and an increase in the size of the valves.

If money was a reason Marr was let go, why did Buick then hire Richard? One possible answer is David decided he would concentrate only on engines, not automobiles – and Richard best reflected the talents he wanted.

According to Hulse, David was at this time experimenting with various types of gasoline engines, trying to perfect one he could make and sell. Richard, after working with Buick's experiments for a few months, decided they were a waste of time. He told Buick he would design a gasoline engine with a new idea that would work. On February 18, 1902, Richard filed for a patent on an overhead-valve gasoline engine, and also for patents on an electric sparker and a carburetor, all assigned to Buick Manufacturing Company.

Dunham, who studied Richard's tortuous path through the patent system, points out the application process began by November 29, 1901. The application was rejected by the patent examiner three times (the biggest problem was it originally included a claim for a water-jacketed valve guide that was found in conflict with earlier patents) Patent rights were assigned to Buick Motor Company on April 4, 1904, by Richard, who had temporarily left the firm. The amended patent was granted to the Buick firm on September 27, 1904.

Richard's patent, number 771,095, covers, among other features, "the combination with the cylinder head, of induction and deduction valves having their stems projecting outward through said head." The construction described is "especially designed with a view to simplicity and ease in manufacture and also the facility with which the parts may be assembled or detached when necessary."

Richard's son, Eugene D. Richard, interviewed in his 80s by the writer, said he once asked his father if he had invented the engine. The father replied he could not understand why "everyone was so interested in that" – the design actually came from steam engines in Europe. He said he "just applied it to the Buick engine."

That checks out with Charles Hulse's recollection of talks with Richard's relatives. Hulse said Richard remembered some steam engines in his native France had used an overhead-valve feature and he merely applied the principle to a gasoline engine he was working on at

'Valve-in-head' engines

Buick. It appears no one before Richard had ever applied for a patent on an overhead-valve engine. (But there's also no evidence the company ever tried to enforce any claim to overhead-valve technology.)

Another checkmark for Richard is a statement by early Buick financier Benjamin Briscoe Jr. Briscoe, himself an auto pioneer who knew Richard well, described Richard as a "mechanical genius" and said that in his opinion the industry owed credit to Richard for "the original proper application of the overhead-valve principle."

But when Walter Marr was once asked to comment on Arthur Pound's statement in *The Turning Wheel* that Richard was largely responsible for Buick's overhead-valve engine, Marr responded: "What he (Pound) didn't say is that I made the valve-in-head device first because it was the easiest way to make a motorcycle engine."

Motorcycle may be a reference to Marr's motor tricycle. In interviews decades later, he said he made his 1899 motor tricycle with the valves in the head "because it had to be built that way." Marr's claim is supported by his personal credibility and track record and by the 1899 news item, quoted previously, that mentions the engine's "very small size."

Terry Dunham believes Marr designed the one-cylinder engine around the tricycle itself. Positioning valves inside the block would have made it too big. "So he mounted the valve train outside the engine. And in the process he made a smaller engine possible, and he also made the first overhead-valve engine built here in the U.S.A.," Dunham once wrote.

But the reference to Marr being first was made before Buick researchers were aware the air-cooled 1902 Franklin used overhead valves based on an engine created by John Wilkinson in 1898. Even if Marr's tricycle did have overhead valves, whether he took that design with him to Buick is not clear. Later, in 1900-01, when Marr built his one-cylinder automobile for Buick, it almost certainly did not have an overhead-valve engine. Marr would have said so if it had.

Marr's next car after the first Buick was a model built for the American Motor Carriage Company (1901-02) in Cleveland. It was called the "American Gas" and Bill Close believes it was copied from the first Buick and used a similar engine. While the first Buick does not exist, an American Gas is in a museum. Its engine has a poppet-valve intake and its exhaust valve is mounted overhead (above the piston). It's not a fully overhead-valve design, so Close believes the first Buick wasn't either.

Marr's relationship with American Motor Carriage lasted only about six months. Marr had been hired August 7, 1901, as chief designer and superintendent with the purpose of building an automobile. The first American Gas was on the road by December 1901. Although the first cars performed well, they failed to attract financing. Production was to be 200 per year but never reached that goal and the American Gas was out of production by 1904. The number built is unknown.

During his tenure at Cleveland, Marr once again displayed both his confidence in his own mechanical ability and his sometimes difficult nature. He was installing a coil in his first American Gas when his boss told him he had a coil in his office he was going to use in the car. Marr's response: "Why didn't you build the car then yourself?"

For whatever reason, Marr soon sensed he would be let go once the car got into production. So he demanded $100 and his car back, and returned to Detroit in February, 1902.

Meanwhile, as Eugene Richard plugged along in his quest to patent the Buick overhead-valve design, a task that spanned about 2 1/2 years, his boss, David Buick, was reorganizing. After David created Buick Manufacturing Company in late 1901 or 1902, and moved operations to Howard Street, Walter Marr returned briefly. He told one interviewer he worked for Buick three times, and each time the company had a different name (that would be Buick Auto-Vim and Power, Buick Manufacturing and Buick Motor).

From Charles Hulse's notes hand written immediately after his 1934 interview of Marr: "(Marr) Went to work for Buick again who was building stationary motors. At the time he started work they were (having) much carburetor trouble, and one day Marr was in the basement and had a carburetor running on the gas and Buick came up to him asking what he was doing and Marr explained that the carbure-

'Valve-in-head' engines

William B. Close

This 1901-02 American Motor Carriage Company vehicle, called the 'American Gas,' is believed to have been copied almost exactly from the first Buick automobile.

tors were leaky and he was trying to find the trouble. Buick intimated that Marr was wasting his (Buick's) money so after a few words Marr again left Buick's employ."

It may be significant Marr worked briefly for Buick Manufacturing Company upon his return to Detroit in early 1902. That was probably the only time Marr, Richard and David Buick worked together in the formative years – a moment when Marr could have learned about Richard's overhead-valve design. Perhaps he could have even helped improve it.

But there is no record that happened. What is certain is that less than a year after Buick, Richard and Marr worked together, both Marr and Buick Motor Company separately developed overhead-valve engines.

Marr designed an innovative overhead-valve/overhead-cam one-cylinder engine for his Marr Autocar that was running by Christmas 1902. Buick Manufacturing Company displayed overhead-valve stationary engines in its catalog probably printed sometime during

71

David Buick's Marvelous Motor Car

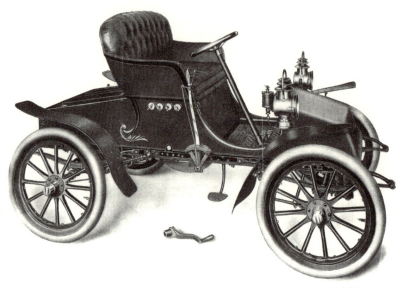

William B. Close

Marr Autocar of 1902-03 had overhead-valve/overhead-cam one-cylinder engine.

1902. It was not until the spring of 1904, however, that Buick Motor Company began to sell its opposed two-cylinder overhead-valve Model B auto engine – perfected just before Marr returned to Buick for the third and last time.

Incidentally, after his split with the American Motor Carriage Company in February 1902, Marr had successfully demanded the return of his car – the first Buick automobile. He brought it back from Cleveland to Detroit and continued to tinker with it.

The car was apparently one hot horseless carriage in Detroit in the early days of the 20th century. Marr said a policeman stopped him three times in one block for driving 20 miles an hour. And once, after he was ticketed for speeding, the arresting officer told the judge Marr was "doing 16 miles an hour with plenty to spare." How he measured the speed is unknown, but the fine was $25. Marr told the judge "the jig is up" – a fine that size would put him out of business. "Your car made 16 miles an hour?" the judge exclaimed. "Well, any man who builds something that'll run that fast deserves better treatment." He

'Valve-in-head' engines

reduced the fine to $2.*

After leaving Buick again, Marr hooked up with J. P. Schneider, a Detroit auto dealer, and began development of the Marr Autocar. Bill Close believes the Marr car (late 1902), like the American Gas, was similar in appearance and many other ways to the first Buick. But it has one major difference, the previously mentioned overhead-valve/ overhead-cam engine.

This was an exceptionally fine roadster and a contract was made with Fauber Manufacturing Company of Elgin, Ill., to begin production.

However, Marr walked away in October 1903, disgusted that Fauber could not keep production on schedule, among other concerns. (Hulse said Marr told him the organizers wanted to get control of the patents but Marr had been "smart enough to have patented his plans so the deal was off.") After perhaps 25 Marr cars were delivered, the company was finished off with a fire in the Elgin factory in August of 1904 that destroyed 14 more. By then, Marr was long gone. In fact, he was back building Buicks, although that's getting ahead of the story.

While the Marr Autocar was apparently not the first American automobile with an overhead-valve engine – the Franklin, for one, may have gone into production some months earlier in 1902 – the Marr car likely arrived before the first overhead-valve Buick car. Buick Motor Company first placed its two-cylinder overhead-valve engine in a Buick automobile when it began producing Model B cars in the summer of 1904 (though some of its new engines may have been fitted a little earlier into other makes). Richard probably should be credited for the one-cylinder engine in a prototype auto – the so-called "Briscoe Buick" – built by David Buick in 1902-03. It was most likely an L-head but even if it did have an overhead-valve engine, it was completed after the first Marr car.

Tracking the early development of Buick's valve-in-head engine

---

* In various interviews, Marr seems to refer to different vehicles, usually his first motor wagon or the first Buick, in telling this story. Charles Hulse's interview notes are a clear reference to the first Buick.

is fascinating to some because it was so critical to Buick Motor Company's early success, and therefore to the creation of General Motors. But perhaps those who ignore the details and simply spread credit for bringing the overhead-valve design to Buick among David Buick, Eugene Richard and Walter Marr have the most accurate answer.

Certainly David Buick was in charge when the design was introduced at Buick. Marr, Richard and Buick all had strong credentials in inventiveness. They could have worked together, building off each other's ideas – and what they may have learned about the overhead valve design in Europe – to create an extraordinary engine design and then developed it separately. But if they did work on it together, they didn't talk about it.

Bill Close believes Marr "built a valve-in-head engine before (David) Buick, Richard and the other automobile manufacturers" and said Marr's "success at building his own car with an overhead-cam and overhead-valve engine in 1902 is proof enough." His position is that Marr's many patents and long and successful career as Buick chief engineer and then consulting engineer are evidence enough of his genius.

GM engineer Kevin Kirbitz, an enthusiast of vintage Buicks, was asked by the writer for his opinions based on his engineering background as well as his historical research.

Kirbitz's viewpoint is that while it's clear overhead-valve placement was "a key enabler" in increasing engine horsepower and efficiency, full credit for the concept cannot be given to any one individual – not David Buick, not Walter Marr, not Eugene Richard.

"In looking at the early development of gasoline engines, it's almost impossible to credit just one person with the development of any particular feature," he said. "Even when the paper trail of patents exists, there was so much simple trial-and-error experimentation that led to true technological breakthrough that it's hard to say who did what and when."

The development of overhead-valve engines was, he said, "a logical and evolutionary step but certainly not ground-breaking." He noted that when William Davis, who patented a water-cooled valve

'Valve-in-head' engines

guide in 1896, used a drawing that clearly showed overhead valves, "he apparently didn't think it novel enough to make a claim." And Kirbitz pointed out that John Wilkinson, the Franklin engineer who designed an overhead-valve engine in 1898, "thought it was the only logical placement for the valves." Walter Marr said he built his 1899 tricycle with valves in the head "because it had to be built that way." And Eugene Richard said he simply applied an existing concept to the Buick engine.

Kirbitz said the question that concerned him was that, given the "nonchalant attitude of these overhead-valve pioneers," why did Buick – and only Buick – so heavily promote "valve-in-head" engines? Finally he decided the Buick engine really was superior, but for other factors in addition to overhead valves. Also, the Buick people – particularly David Buick, Walter Marr and Eugene Richard – came to understand the significance of the design. And once that significance was explained to Durant, the super salesman wasted little time promoting the Buick engine.

Said Kirbitz: "The evidence indicates that Buick, as depicted in the Richard engine patent, was the first manufacturer to successfully integrate all of the elements of what is today commonly regarded as the overhead-valve engine, including valve placement, valve-train operation and engine cooling. It is this combination of ideas which set the Buick engine apart from its contemporaries."

An opinion on the specific roles of the individuals will not be ventured here. But Kirbitz's statement above is, in the writer's opinion, a good overall summation. The bottom line: Buick's new engine *was* extraordinary – and it would provide the momentum for decades of outstanding success.

Valve-in-Head: Technology in Historical Perspective

The writer is a Buick historian by hobby and a General Motors engineer by profession. He began his GM career with Buick in 1979 and is still involved in the development of future Buick products. These observations were written especially for this publication.

By KEVIN M. KIRBITZ

With so much early emphasis placed on Buick's prominence as a pioneer builder of valve-in-head engines, it's helpful to have a basic understanding of what this meant in those early years of automotive development.

The dawn of the 20th century was an era in which many automotive-related debates were still raging. Should steam, electricity or an internal combustion engine be used for motive power? If it's an internal combustion engine, should it be fueled by alcohol, benzene or gasoline? Should the engine be cooled by air or water? Which ignition system – hot tube, hammer spark or jump spark – was best? What was the best location for the intake and exhaust valves and how should they be operated?

In a four-cycle internal combustion engine, intake valves allow the air and fuel mixture to enter the combustion chamber and, after combustion has occurred, exhaust valves allow the burned gases to escape into the atmosphere. When David Buick began experimenting with gasoline engines, several different valve configurations were in common use. Most valves were set in chambers along the side of the cylinder head, and operated in a line parallel to the piston. Examples can be found in early Locomobile and Stevens-Duryea engines.

This arrangement was a predecessor to what is today known as an L-head (with valves placed in chambers along the same side of the cylinder) or a T-head (with valves placed in chambers on opposite sides of the cylinder). On other engines, such as the Oldsmobile and Cadillac single-cylinder models, valves operated perpendicular to the piston in a chamber projecting from the top of the cylinder head. Engines with both valves located directly in the cylinder head above the piston eventually became known as overhead valve (ohv), or, as Buick would advertise the design for some 50 years, "Valve-in-Head."

Although the engine and features patented by Eugene Richard for Buick are unquestionably an overhead-valve design, it must

Valve-in-Head: Technology in Historical Perspective

also be said that overhead valves were not unique to Buick. Such valves were commonly used in steam engines during this period, and there were instances of internal-combustion engines in Europe which also used the design.

The illustration for an 1896 U.S. patent held by William F. Davis clearly shows valves located in the cylinder head. Davis's patentable claim, however, was for a water jacket surrounding the valve stems and valve guides, not necessarily for valve placement. The Davis engine designs were noted for their simplicity as well, and in 1902 his company merged with the Waterloo Gasoline Engine Company, which manufactured the now famous Waterloo Boy tractor, predecessor of John Deere.

In 1898, John Wilkinson, who had attended Cornell University, built a four-cylinder, air-cooled, overhead-valve engine using atmospheric intake valves. After an initial investment deal to manufacture the Wilkinson automobile failed, the talented engineer joined forces with financial backer and industrialist Herbert H. Franklin and in 1902 began manufacture of the Franklin motor car. Unlike Buick, the Franklin firm never said much about overhead valves because, from Wilkinson's point of view, there was no other logical place for valves to be located.

In Indianapolis, Ind., Howard Marmon, a graduate of the University of California Berkeley, was chief engineer at his family's flour mill machinery business when he built his first experimental automobile in 1902. His engine was an air-cooled V-twin featuring overhead valves and a pressure lubrication system. Marmon went on to produce a V-4 powered vehicle in 1903 and six more in 1904. Full-scale production began in 1905 with 25 cars. By 1909, Marmon had abandoned air cooling for water cooling and switched from V-type to inline cylinder arrangements. For a time (1909-1915), Marmon also switched from overhead valves to a T-head design, but returned to overhead valves after that.

Valve placement in these early four-cycle engines had a lot to do with the way the valves were opened and closed. Exhaust valves were typically operated through a positive mechanical linkage tied to the engine's camshaft through push rods. This allows precise timing of exhaust valve operation during the four-cycle process (intake, compression, power, and exhaust).

On the other hand, intake valves, including those on some early Buick stationary engines, were called atmospheric valves. The atmospheric intake valves were opened by the suction produced by the downward motion of the piston, and were closed with a return spring. Because the operation of an atmospheric valve is not precisely timed to the combustion cycle, efficient operation was sometimes sporadic. To compound the problems, atmospheric valves were sometimes prone to sticking and varying spring tension could further hinder efficient intake-valve operation.

If internal combustion engines were to advance, the problem of the atmospheric valve had to be addressed. Although some manufacturers had experimented with a positive mechanical linkage for intake-valve actuation, the idea still defied the conventional wisdom of the period. In the 1905 edition of *Self Propelled Vehicles* by James E. Homans, a section devoted to inlet valves noted that "experience has taught that the positive cam-actuating inlet valve is not nearly as efficient as the older forms." The text continued by saying that in "the positive valve type, it is necessary . . . to allow a large compression space in the head, which absolutely reduces compression in itself and causes a loss of power."

Such was the case with early L-head Ford and Packard engines which used positive inlet valves. In these as well as in T-head engines, the additional volume required for the valve chambers reduced the amount of compression the piston could exert on the air/fuel mixture, which lessened the heat output of combustion, and resulted in a loss of power. In liquid-cooled engines, larger cooling jacket space led to even more heat loss and even further power loss.

In contrast, the Buick stationary engine, as described in the Richard patent application, employed valves located in the cylinder head above the piston, requiring no additional space for valve chambers. Furthermore, both exhaust and inlet valves were positively operated through pushrods, driven by a camshaft, so their operation could be consistently and precisely timed. Richard and Buick had very effectively defied the conventional wisdom. The design was also adapted to Buick's first two-cylinder automobile engine in 1904. Other manufacturers would follow, including Franklin, which abandoned the atmospheric valve in 1905 in favor of the pushrod and rocker arm design.

Richard's patent specifically noted simplicity and ease of manufacture, assembly and disassembly as benefits for locating the valves in the cylinder head. No mention was made of any inherent increase in power due to valve placement. One of the earli-

Valve-in-Head: Technology in Historical Perspective

est Buick Motor Company catalogs, probably published in 1904, said the company's aim was to "make our engine as simple and as easy to understand as possible, hence our reason for putting all the working parts on the outside."

By 1905, possibly as a result of deductive reasoning and a series of crude dynamometer tests, Buick had discovered that overhead valves allowed the engine to breathe better and the air/fuel mixture to burn faster, resulting in more horsepower per cubic inch of displacement than engines using other valve configurations. Due in large part to the solid reputation of the Buick engine and an extensive advertising campaign which presented the benefits of "valve-in-head," it wasn't long until the public began to think of Buick's valve-in-head engines as being among the very best available.

Yet not all early Buick cars used overhead valve. When the four-cylinder Model D was introduced in 1906, the catalog pointed out "the inlet and outlet valves are on opposite sides of the cylinder," clearly a T-head design. In 1908, Buick introduced the Model 5 as a four-cylinder L-head. The 1909 Model 6 and the 1909-1910 Buick Model 41 limousines also had non-overhead-valve engines. Fortunately, the famous and highly successful Model 10, introduced in 1908, used a new four-cylinder engine with "valve in the head construction."

In the ensuing years, and probably due at least in part to the opening of a new engine plant in 1909, Buick turned almost exclusively to the overhead valve design. The sole exception was the 1930 Buick Marquette, which used a six-cylinder L-head.

Said to be the United States' greatest technological contribution to World War I, the Liberty aircraft engine used an overhead-valve design and the sales people at Buick were quick to make the point. The Liberty engine design program had been led by E. J. Hall of the Hall-Scott Motor Company, a manufacturer of aircraft engines, and J. G. Vincent, the chief engineer at Packard Motor Company. Packard had previous experience building V-12 automotive engines.

Buick became involved early on as one of seven automobile manufacturers contracted by the government to build the Liberty, and Buick is believed to have built the first experimental Liberty V-8 engines, which preceded the V-12s. Although it is unclear what role Buick may have played in choosing the overhead-valve configuration for the Liberty, for several months after Armistice Day,

David Buick's Marvelous Motor Car

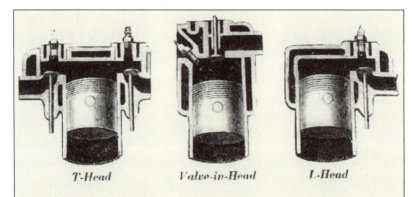

T-Head   Valve-in-Head   L-Head

Buick boldly advertised its role in their production, claiming that, as valve-in-head engines, they were "unequalled in their power to weight ratios."

Over time, the overhead-valve engine became the standard for gasoline engines throughout the world. Notably, GM's 3800 Series III V-6, an overhead-valve, pushrod engine still in production at the time of this writing, traces its design heritage back to Buick's first V-8 engines built in 1953, and its engineering DNA back to the inventive minds of David Buick, Eugene Richard, and Walter Marr. An award-winning engine, the 3800 is today capable of delivering more than 30 miles per gallon, with more than 200 horsepower, and is designated as a Super Low Emission Vehicle (SULEV) engine. The plant in north Flint where the 3800 is built is the last production facility on the site of Buick's home complex, developed early in the 20th century by Billy Durant.

In looking at the early development of gasoline engines, it's almost impossible to credit just one person with the development of any particular feature. Even when the paper trail of patents exists, there was so much simple trial-and-error experimentation that led to true technological breakthrough that it's hard to say exactly who did what and when. The evidence would, however, support Buick as the first manufacturer to successfully integrate the elements of what is known today as the overhead-valve engine.

By discovering the benefits of the overhead-valve design in the formative years of the automotive industry, and through years of continued refinement and improvement, Buick gained a crucial competitive advantage in engine development and forever solidified its place in history as the "Pioneer Builder of Valve-in-Head Motor Cars."

Chapter 8

Buick starts a new company

When he offered to sell his carriage bodies to Walter Marr in 1901, David Buick appeared to be giving up on automobiles to concentrate on engines. After all, Marr was the man who could put an entire vehicle together, and now he was gone. But the carriage bodies went unsold, at least to Marr, and by 1902 David was back at it – working on an automobile said to be of his own design.

At the same time, he continued to work on his engine designs, presumably with Eugene Richard. One of his consistent messages was simplicity of engine design, a common theme among engine builders of the time.

Buick Manufacturing's first catalog, probably dating to 1902, also boasts of the best mechanics, the best steel and that "each engine is an advertisement in itself." It makes a big quality claim for the time: "All parts…are interchangeable." It also makes a big claim for fame. Its cover is decorated with a drawing of Uncle Sam pulling a Buick engine on a cart – called "on truck" – across the globe, accompanied with a slogan: "Known All Over the World." (He would keep that design on several future catalogs.)

The catalog discusses overhead valve engines: "The inlet and outlet valves are in the head…so should it become necessary to grind or reseat the valves it would not be necessary to take the entire engine to a machine shop…but simply take the head…" There was no claim of a power advantage.

By late 1902, as he struggled to build an automobile, David found himself in debt for several hundred dollars to Benjamin Briscoe Jr., who operated a big sheet metal business in Detroit and who was learning how to build radiators and other automotive equipment.

Briscoe did not push to collect. After all, he noted, "David

Buick and I were old friends from before the automobile business was thought of in Detroit." Buick was "a personal friend and a fine chap generally, and ... I appreciated his having always given me all the business he could in his former company (Buick & Sherwood), which amounted to many thousands of dollars a year."

He explained: "We (Briscoe) were galvanizing and sheet metal workers and Mr. Buick's business of manufacturing plumbers' suppliers required such services as we rendered." Not only that, Briscoe said, after Buick began building stationary engines, he continued to buy a good deal of material from Briscoe "and in that way our business association was maintained."

Buick was undeterred by his inability to pay his debts to Briscoe (and apparently to others). In fact, he was seeking more money so he could complete his automobile. Unwilling to give up that dream, he invited Briscoe to his factory, showed him his unfinished car and asked for more help.

"He told me his troubles and how impossible it was for him to pay me or in fact to pay any one of his creditors at that time," Briscoe recalled. "The reason he gave me was that he had invested most of his capital and 'then some' in a design for an automobile. In fact he showed me that if he could not refinance himself through the medium of this automobile, he would not be able to pay anyone."

Briscoe, intrigued rather than angered, agreed to advance $650 to finish the automobile – but the car would then be his. "I proposed that, as I did not own a car, that I buy the car they were working on, furnishing them money to complete it. I had to furnish a good deal more money that I had anticipated."

When Briscoe planned a long visit to France in the summer of 1903 to study building radiators, Buick became "disturbed," to quote Briscoe. One imaginative source said Buick pleaded: "What am I going to do, Ben?" Briscoe: "I don't know, Dave. You'll have to blow up, I guess. I can't stand any more of this." Buick said he needed more money to "carry on." They finally agreed Buick could survive with $1,500 more for the interim.

So Briscoe proposed a seemingly odd deal. Briscoe would lend

Buick starts a new company

the $1,500, which meant Buick's total debt to Briscoe would be about $3,500. In return, Buick would incorporate his company with a capital of $100,000, "mostly represented by patents and inventions," Briscoe suggested, and transfer most stock to Briscoe. Buick could redeem the stock by fall by simply paying Briscoe the $3,500 he was owed, or Briscoe would take over the company. David Buick agreed.

The firm was incorporated under the name Buick Motor Company May 19, 1903. David Buick had 9,499 shares, son Thomas Buick 500, and Emil D. Moessner, Briscoe's son-in-law, one share. Moessner was probably there to keep an eye on Briscoe's interests, because Briscoe was in control (though his name does not show up in the incorporation papers). The incorporation date has been used by Buick Motor Division over the years as its official birth date.*

Even after the new company was created, the previous Buick firm stayed in existence for a brief period. Four days after Buick Motor Company's incorporation, Eugene Richard signed a two-year contract with Buick Manufacturing Company as "designer and inventor and head of drafting department" for a starting salary of $100 a month. Under the contract, on January 1, 1904, Richard would have the option of a $25-a-month salary increase or taking $2,500 in stock received from the sale of property and assets of Buick Manufacturing Company to Buick Motor Company.

The contract was probably created to build credibility for Buick Motor Company's $100,000 capitalization by securing the firm's rights to Richard's patents and inventions. The contract stated Richard "further agrees to apply for patents when requested to do so," to

---

* When the writer was privileged to join a small group that previewed a Ken Burns TV special in 2002 at Burns' farmhouse studio in New Hampshire, a coincidence was pointed out. The date of Buick Motor Company's incorporation – May 19, 1903 – is also remembered in automotive history for another event. That very night in the University Club in San Francisco, Horatio Nelson Jackson, a 31-year-old doctor from Vermont, made a bet he could drive an automobile from San Francisco to New York City in less than three months. Four days later, he set out in a Winton in an epic story told in the book, *Horatio's Drive,* by Dayton Duncan and Ken Burns. It was the story of America's first cross-country road trip, which became the television program of the same name previewed in that New Hampshire farmhouse.

apply for patents on all inventions he had already made "in this line" and to assign such applications or patents to Buick. (The original of that document was given by Richard's son to the writer for the Buick archives in the mid 1990s). As it turned out, Richard did not stay with Buick long enough to take advantage of the optional increases – he left in September of 1903.

About the time Buick Motor Company was created, Briscoe began to consider whether he wanted to work with a more experienced auto man, Jonathan D. Maxwell, and clean up the Buick business and move on. He perceived that Maxwell, who had collaborated with the Apperson brothers, Elwood Haynes, Ransom E. Olds and other pioneer auto designers, was way ahead of the curve when compared with David Buick.

It also helped that Maxwell and Olds had visited Briscoe's office in 1902 with an engine "cooler" (radiator) they wanted him to build. When Briscoe returned with a satisfactory sample, Olds and Maxwell ordered 4,400 of them, along with an equal number of tanks, sets of fenders and other sheet metal parts. This was a big order in the earliest days of the Detroit auto business. If David Buick was a good customer, Maxwell was now an even better one.

Briscoe described Maxwell as a man with "an enviable and successful record" who was also endowed "with a high degree of common sense along with which he had practical knowledge, exceptionally broad at that time, applying to automobiles." Briscoe sent Maxwell to check out David Buick's operations. It's probably fair to say Maxwell was not impressed. Briscoe insisted Maxwell didn't say anything favorable or unfavorable about the Buick proposition. But pointedly, Maxwell wondered if Briscoe would like to "hook up" with him in the automobile business.

That sounded good to Briscoe. He shifted gears quickly. By July 4, 1903, he was already backing Maxwell in development of a Maxwell car, and Briscoe would organize the Maxwell-Briscoe Company in the fall of the year. But at the same time, Briscoe was now owner of the second car to carry the Buick name, and the first apparently designed by David Buick.

Buick starts a new company

Benjamin Briscoe, Jr.

Although Briscoe would later boast he started Buick Motor Company, which is close to true, he didn't claim much of a hand in the car itself. Writing to the editor of *The Automobile* magazine in 1915, he acknowledged: "As to what part I played in the laying out of the first Buick car, I cannot say I did much of anything with reference to design, except to make general suggestions and recommendations during the progress of the work."

He recalled "the motor had exceptionally large valves, was a single cylinder motor of about 4 x 5...and did develop by brake test about 26 H.P., which was quite marvelous at the time for that size motor, in fact would be a good performance even for today...."

Briscoe's recollection is likely wrong. If the engine really was a one-cylinder, it would have generated less horsepower. Charles Hulse states without listing a source that the Briscoe Buick's one-cylinder engine developed 7 horsepower.

If it had been an overhead-valve engine, Briscoe and Hulse most

David Buick's Marvelous Motor Car

likely would have so noted. The record, however, is not clear. Buick wasn't building overhead-valve engines for automobiles in 1903. However, a year earlier, Buick Manufacturing Company noted its four-cycle stationary engine, which had an overhead-valve design, could "be adapted to automobile purposes, with a few simple changes." Still, as mentioned earlier, the prevailing opinion is David Buick probably used an L-head engine in this vehicle. The overhead-valve Buick auto engine was coming, but not until the beginning of 1904.

The Briscoe company built so many parts for the car they were "too numerous to mention," Briscoe said, but they did include all of the sheet metal as well as machine work on small parts.

Briscoe was adamant about one thing – Marr had nothing to do with this Buick automobile. "I do not recall that I ever saw Mr. Marr there" while it was being designed, he said. Of course he would have known Marr was then developing the Marr Autocar, because Briscoe was also providing many parts for that vehicle.

Briscoe drove David Buick's car for several months and "discovered most of the bugs that were in it…I was part of the experimental department and as such had many strenuous experiences." This automobile was registered as the "Bewick" in Detroit on January 24, 1904, shortly after a city ordinance was passed in Detroit, in advance of the state, requiring that cars be registered. It was assigned license number 365.

Briscoe understood David Buick's passion for automobiles. He was hooked as well, and so could describe the feeling. Buick, said Briscoe, had "gotten the automobile bee in his bonnet, and it is my experience…that when a man became infected with the automobile germ, it was as though he had a disease. It had to run its course. No man in those days would have gone into the automobile business if he had been a hard-boiled conservative business man. It took a man of pioneering instinct, an idealist – of an adventurous nature…."

Briscoe was consistent in his praise of David Buick's abilities. In a 1915 letter, he told D. Beecroft, managing editor of *The Automobile*: "Mr. Buick is a very capable mechanic and I understand he has lately developed a very excellent carburetor."

But Briscoe was quite straightforward in his plans regarding

Buick starts a new company

This is believed to be the second experimental Buick automobile. It was designed and built in Buick Manufacturing's plant on Howard Street in Detroit by David Buick in 1902-03 and sold to Benjamin Briscoe Jr., his Detroit financial angel. The 'Briscoe Buick' was a factor in the sale of Buick Motor Company to the Flint Wagon Works directors in fall 1903. This poor quality photo from a newspaper is the only known possible likeness of the car.

Buick and Maxwell. Briscoe wrote that if he and Buick were unable to sell the firm, and Briscoe was unable to get his money back, he would then "buy out Mr. Buick and have Mr. Maxwell use the Buick shop as a nucleus for a plant in which to produce the Maxwell car."

In the summer of 1903, neither Briscoe nor Maxwell fully understood what David Buick and his team had wrought with Buick's powerful new engine design. Buick Motor Company didn't seem too sure, either. The catalog copy on overhead-valve engines – identified by description because that label had yet to be invented – still boasted only of ease of servicing, not power. And, as noted, the design had yet to be specifically adapted by Buick to an automobile.

Soon that would all change. Jacob H. Newmark, one of Durant's advertising men, commenting from the perspective of 1936, best summed up Buick's No. 1 achievement.

"The Buick Motor Company prospered…almost from the beginning, and all because the company was unusually fortunate in its en-

From the Richard family album: Above, Eugene Richard about the time of his marriage (left) and as a young engineer (right). Below, Eugene and Louisa Richard in later years at their Flint home.

gine design," Newmark wrote. "Buick, without doubt, had one of the best of the early engines. It would go and keep on going. Roads were of all kinds in those days – most of them sand, clay and what-not. Buick's early valve-in-head motor did have power if nothing else, and the new car would negotiate all sorts of road conditions...The fame of the new motor grew steadily."

David Buick was confident he had good engines. But in the summer of 1903, nobody could have guessed where they would take him.

Chapter 9

Move to Flint

With an incorporated company, a catalog of superior engines and one car to show off, Buick in the summer of 1903 had a package that might sell. And sure enough, it did. The opportunity came from a surprising place – Flint, Michigan, a city of about 14,000, some 60 miles north of Detroit. Dwight Stone, a real estate salesman in Flint, tipped Benjamin Briscoe's brother Frank, who was visiting relatives in the city, that the Flint Wagon Works was looking to buy into an engine company and possibly build automobiles. That's the story as related in Flint.

Ben Briscoe tells it slightly differently, in a magazine article setting up the story in his meandering style that nearly defeats his attempt at drama: "A thing happened which, though trivial in itself, was one of those happenings that measured by the changes it wrought in the lives of many people, and the fortunes of many men, proved to be one of those 'high spot' occurrences that seem as though they are predestined."

During a conversation with a salesman, Briscoe said he learned a Flint vehicle maker – the Flint Wagon Works – was contemplating the manufacture of automobiles.

"I pricked up my ears, and upon my inquiry as to whether they had a car to manufacture, he said he understood they did not, but that they were looking for one," Briscoe continued. "This, then, was my cue for disposing of the Buick car and getting my money out." The next day he and Frank headed for Flint to meet with James H. Whiting, the firm's president and managing director, and other wagon works directors. "I sold the Flint Wagon Works the Buick car on that day. The deal was not closed then to be sure, as they wanted to see the car and talk to Mr. Buick, but for all intents and purposes they bought it that day."

David Buick's Marvelous Motor Car

James Whiting was a Civil War veteran and onetime owner of a hardware store in downtown Flint who had taken over the Begole, Fox and Company lumber mill in Flint and managed its transition into a successful wagon maker. The Flint Wagon Works became Flint's first incorporated company in 1884. A surviving record book of his expenses paints Whiting as a thoroughly modern businessman, traveling quickly from city to city by train, touching bases with business executives on the road, and riding herd on company expenses. In one later entry he notes a need to talk "about tel. bill of DD Buick."

Whiting was also fascinated with automobiles. When he went to carriage shows, he would join fellow carriage executive A.B.C. Hardy in visiting any auto show nearby. And when Hardy began manufacturing his Hardy Flint Roadster automobiles in Flint in 1901, Whiting would visit his factory. (Hardy built 52 cars from 1901-03). The Buick company, not too expensive to buy, not too far away to visit, must have seemed just what he was looking for. Briscoe wrote: "Although there were some discouraging moments during the negotiations and the attempted trial runs of the car, I could see that nothing except some unexpected turn in events could 'unsell them.' " Charles A. Cumings, superintendent of the Flint Wagon Works, told Hulse he went to Detroit with the Whiting group and that David Buick showed them the Briscoe Buick.

David himself was apparently the source of a story he had to drive the Briscoe Buick to Flint to close the deal. Heading north, the car broke down in Pontiac (between Detroit and Flint) and was towed back with a team of horses. Buick made the trip successfully on his next attempt. This anecdote in a biographical sketch approved by David Buick sounds believable, although it's the only reference anywhere of Buick actually driving one of his experimental cars. Hulse once identified an uncaptioned photo of a car in a largely inaccurate story about Buick in *The Flint Journal* on May 18, 1904, as probably the Briscoe Buick. Its exterior design indicates it had moved further along the styling road from carriage to automobile than either the first Buick or the Marr Autocar.

If Briscoe's and Buick's recollections are correct about Whiting's interest in the Buick automobile, then Whiting was hiding his true intentions from others. His public story was he wanted the Buick firm so he could build engines his salesmen could peddle to farmers for stationary use or to wholesale to auto makers.

The sale of Buick Motor Company to the Flint Wagon Works directors was completed September 3, 1903. Reportedly the deal was cinched for $10,000, which the Flint Wagon Works directors borrowed on a one-year note from the Union Trust & Savings Bank of Flint, guaranteed by the signatures of its five directors – James H. Whiting, Charles M. Begole, George L. Walker, William S. Ballenger and Charles A. Cumings. As early Flint historian Frank Rodolf pointed out, the bank wasn't gambling money on a shaky automotive concern, but making the loan based on the signatures of five very substantial local citizens.

The little city of Flint, incorporated in 1855, could trace its beginnings to 1819 or earlier when a trading post was established by fur trader Jacob Smith on an Indian trail at a shallow crossing of the Flint River. Indians in the Saginaw Valley and northern Michigan who wanted to trade furs could canoe no further south on the river than the site of Flint before they would have to travel 60 miles on foot to the big trading center at Detroit. It was a great place for Smith to set up shop. He could beat the competition and save the Indians the walk. In 1830, John and Polly Todd established a tavern just across the river from Smith's store, guarded by a chained pet bear named Trinc. When social observer/writer Alexis de Tocqueville spent the night at Todd's Tavern on July 24, 1831, as he toured the American wilderness, he noted: "What a devil of a country this is, where one has bears for watchdogs."

Soon a government road was cut through the wilderness from Detroit and a land office opened at Flint. Settlers began to arrive in large numbers to clear the land and create farms. But the most valuable natural resource in the area was the white pine. Large stands of pine along the river north of Flint were soon being cut, with the logs floated to the booms in Flint. There, sawmills created great piles of lumber to build Detroit and Chicago and other cities.

One of the area's biggest lumber barons was Henry Howland

James H. Whiting: He brought Buick to Flint

Crapo (Cray-po), who came from New Bedford, Mass., in January of 1856 to manage timber land for Eastern investors. Crapo built a sawmill and then a railroad. He became mayor of Flint, and then, in the 1860s, governor of Michigan. Twice he met with Abraham Lincoln during the Civil War. Occasionally he sent letters to his young grandson, Willie Durant, who lived with his parents in Boston and would someday move to Flint, save Buick and create General Motors.

By 1903, when Buick came to town, Flint was already known as "The Vehicle City." The name had nothing to do with automobiles. A local judge, Charles Wisner, had built several horseless carriages – the first as early as 1898 – and one former carriage maker, A.B.C. Hardy, was, as mentioned, producing a runabout named the Hardy Flint Roadster in small numbers. But The Vehicle City was an acknowledgment of such carriage and wagon firms as the William A. Paterson Carriage Works, Flint Wagon Works, W. F. Stewart Company and the storied Durant-Dort Carriage Company (which alone produced 50,000 vehicles a year by 1901). When one of the carriage leaders made a decisive step, the banks, the business leaders and local newspapers took notice.

Whiting's announcement that the Flint Wagon Works directors had bought Buick Motor Company was therefore the top news story in *The Flint Journal* on September 11, 1903. (It shared Page One with a story about a state conference of horse shoers –a case of transportation eras passing). Whiting said ground had been broken that morning for a 200x65-foot factory on W. Kearsley Street on the west side of Flint near the wagon works. The newspaper described Buick as a "splendid new manufacturing industry" and it certainly sounded that way. Whiting said the new company had paid-in capital stock of $50,000, would hire 100 skilled mechanics and machinists and would manufacture stationary and marine engines, automobile engines, transmissions, carburetors and "sparking plugs."

Whiting was asked by a reporter to comment on a rumor the company would also build automobiles. He smiled at the question and replied the "broader opportunity" would be considered later.

The Flint Journal in an editorial the next day was both enthusiastic and prophetic. And it pushed Whiting to go further than his announcement:

> Flint is the most natural center for the manufacture of autos in the whole country. It is the vehicle city of the United States and in order to maintain this name by which it is known from ocean to ocean there must be developed factories here for the manufacture of…automobiles. *The Journal* believes that the time is not very far away when every part connected with an auto will be manufactured here and when an immense industry will have been developed.

David said he tried to find money to keep his plant in Detroit but was unsuccessful.

Flint in 1903 (above), when Buick came to town. Some of the city's famous arches were erected in 1901 but the 'Vehicle City' arch (below) was created in 1905 for Flint's Golden Jubilee. The arches came down just after World War I, but when new ones were erected early in the new millennium, Buick Motor Division sponsored one – though Buick had recently been moved by GM to Detroit.

"For two years we have been located at 416-418 Howard Street and the business has grown until orders for $185,000 are on the books which we are unable to fill. It became absolutely necessary to enlist more capital, but no substantial encouragement was made in Detroit."

Discussing the move, he said about 30 employees would move to Flint but didn't sound very excited about personally relocating. "I shall necessarily be compelled to make my home there although Detroit seems to me a very desirable place for a residence."

Buick's departure from Detroit was not unnoticed. *The Detroit Journal* interviewed J. B. Howarth, said to be "one of the most level-headed businessmen" of Detroit, who commented:

> If Mr. Buick has been looking around for additional capital during the last six months, he did so at the wrong time. The banks and those who have the means to invest in such enterprises are now retrenching instead of expanding.
>
> The tightness in the money market has brought about a feeling of conservation. But a year ago, and before that for several years, I heard of no well-organized industry, or any industry that could show a healthy condition, failing to get all the capital it needed in Detroit.
>
> (Flint) is off the main lines of road and is obligated to offer special attractions to individual concerns to induce them to locate there. The fact that we as a city lose an industry to a smaller city in the same state does not appear to me as a very great injury, for the merchants of Flint who will be benefited…depend largely on Detroit wholesalers and manufacturers for their supplies.

Howarth's opinion that "Mr. Buick has been trying to do the right thing at the wrong time" revealed ignorance of David's need for quick action to avoid Briscoe's takeover of his company.

Eugene Richard did not follow Buick to Flint. In September 1903 he accepted more money to return to the Kneeland Crystal Creamery, his old employer in Lansing. It wanted him to design a new gas engine for its cream separator. On December 30, 1903, he filed for

Flint Wagon Works: Its directors bought Buick in 1903, set it up in new factory nearby.

a patent on a gasoline stationary engine that was assigned to Sarah L. Kneeland, widow of C. L. Kneeland. By then, Richard had already moved to another Lansing firm, Peerless Motor Company, as designer and draftsman. (He was promoted to superintendent in 1906 but on June 27, 1908, he returned to Buick in Flint as designer/draftsman in the engineering department. He was granted seven patents, all assigned to Buick, between 1912 and 1919.)

Briscoe returned from Europe in the fall of 1903 and learned the sale of Buick Motor Company to the Flint Wagon Works directors was complete. He said David Buick called immediately and "justified my high opinion of his integrity as he 'came through' handsomely, paying me interest on the money and a bonus in addition."

All of this new-found money and the prospect of a new factory emboldened the company. On October 21, 1903, Tom Buick wrote to a boat manufacturer in an unrecorded but presumably far-away city:

> This is no doubt the first time that our name has been brought before you as manufacturers of marine engines...our output was limited, and (we) were able to dispose of all the engines we could manufacture in certain localities...but as we are now building a large and modern plant at Flint, Mich., it becomes necessary for us to extend our territory, and increase our sales to take care of the large output we will have....

He continued that the firm had been manufacturing 2- and 4-horsepower four-cycle engines but was now adding sizes and making a two-cycle marine engine. He boasted Buick's present customers had few complaints and "we are absolutely certain that if you handle our engines your engine troubles will become a thing of the past."

Local newspapers kept up with the factory's progress. By November 18, 1903, exterior work was complete and some machinery had been installed. A reporter commented on its spaciousness: "surprising…and a great deal more than a person would expect…a feature of the construction that has been especially well taken care of has been the matter of light of which there is an abundance."

Even as machinery was being loaded into the plant, work was progressing on a large two-cylinder automobile engine. There were numerous oddities surrounding this engine. First, while it was described as Buick's first two-cylinder auto engine, it was not built for Buick. According to Hulse, who interviewed some of the players, apparently Buick was the prime contractor on producing an engine for the Reid Manufacturing Company, Detroit, for its new Wolverine car to be produced in January of 1904.

Buick had contracted some work on this engine to Peerless Motor Company – and so Eugene Richard, now at Peerless, was involved. Also, Walter Marr was working for Reid in December 1903 and early January 1904 – on the Wolverine automobile. It's likely he would have had input into the engine design. So possibly Richard and Marr, neither at the moment employed by Buick, were helping Buick build an auto engine not for Buick's use.

Hulse interviewed William H. Wascher, a Flint native hired as an electrician at the plant late in 1903. Wascher said the plant, up and running in early December, was making a few marine, stationary and auto engines, all one-cylinder, and assembly was starting on the two-cylinder auto engine for Reid.

Fred Tiedeman, a part-time photographer, was called to the Buick plant and asked to take a photo of this first Reid engine, according to Hulse. Tiedeman was told this was the first two-cylinder engine the Buick company had ever made for an automobile. The photo reveals the engine did not use overhead valves. *Cycle and Automobile Trade Journal* said it "differs from most gasoline engines now on the market in that the engine is placed horizontally under the hood parallel with the axles." The engine, it said, generated 15 horsepower but that could be boosted to 17.5 at a higher rpm.

The factory was in operation by December 5, 1903, with Arthur C. Mason, formerly of Cadillac and recently hired as superintendent of Buick production, in charge of the move from Detroit. On December 11, *The Flint Journal* reported the plant had 25 employees and had made five engines of three-quarters to 13 horsepower. One model was a four-cycle marine engine that, according to Charles Hulse, was invented by Eugene Richard in 1902 and first produced by Buick Manufacturing Company in 1902-03 and then by Buick Motor Company in 1903-04.

The factory force was also starting work on "a huge double-cylinder auto engine," *The Journal* said. This was either the Reid engine or a newly designed powerplant – the soon-to-be-famous Buick Model B. Hulse said the first Model B engine was completed January 4, 1904. The big engines, originally rated at 12 horsepower, went into production in March of 1904 "and were being offered to the various automobile manufacturers at a time when many new organizations were trying to get started in the automobile business," Hulse wrote.

Since neither Richard nor Marr was employed by Buick between September 1903 and March 1904, there's a question of who was designing engines for Buick in that period. One answer is David Buick. But Hulse believed the Model B engine was primarily designed by Buick's two newly hired manufacturing leaders, Arthur Mason and his assistant, William Beacraft. The engine had an overhead-valve design, picked up from the firm's stationary and marine engines that could be traced to Richard or Marr or both.

Fred G. Hoelzle, a longtime Buick superintendent who was 15 in 1901 when he started as a toolroom apprentice at Peerless, was in his 90s when interviewed by the writer in the late 1970s. He also wrote his own manuscripts on his reminiscences. At Peerless, Hoelzle met Richard. This was likely after Richard left Buick, rejoined the Kneeland Crystal Creamery briefly and then went to work for Peerless late in 1903.

Hoelzle remembered Richard was building a two-cycle engine for Peerless and "was also interested in building a motor car for Mr.

Move to Flint

Buick's first two-cylinder auto engine was built in late 1903 for the Reid Company's Wolverine automobile.

Early Buick researcher Charles E. Hulse (left) discusses the Buick stationary engine with William H. Wascher, who was hired as an electrician at the Buick plant when it was built in 1903. The only known stationary Buick Motor Company engine surviving, this one was built in Flint and later sold by Hulse to Harold Warp's Pioneer Village in Minden, Neb.

David Buick's Marvelous Motor Car

Arthur C. Mason (left), Buick engine superintendent, years later with W.C. Durant.

Mason is credited for Buick's two-cylinder overhead-valve automobile engine of 1904.

Move to Flint

David Buick in Detroit. I met his Detroit partner while at Peerless, Mr. Walter Marr, and did some work for him. Mr. Richard…was working on an idea of valve-in-head motors. I machined the valve cage with the valve assembly that…could be removed from (the) cylinder for valve trouble, etc., and again assembled with a simple clamp-tightening process. He was very excited about this….'' Hoelzle must have been helping Richard do Peerless contract work for Buick on the early Buick Model B engine.

The company was soon reorganized. On January 16, 1904, in a meeting in Flint chaired by David Buick, the board dissolved Detroit-born Buick Motor Company. It transferred assets to Whiting to organize a Flint company, same name, incorporated January 30, 1904. Large stockholders were David Buick and son Thomas (1,500 shares between them), Whiting as president (1,504), Charles M. Begole, vice president (1,068), George L. Walker, director (725), and William S. Ballenger, treasurer (707). The officers were the same as for the Flint Wagon Works, except David Buick was secretary of the motor company.

The company's purpose was listed as manufacturer of power machinery, automobile "equipments," automobiles, pumps, engines and other mechanical appliances. The firm was capitalized at $75,000 instead of the $50,000 originally intended, with half, $37,500, paid in.

In what may have been a surprise to Flint investors, David let it be known he could not manage Buick in Flint because he owed $11,000 to creditors in Detroit. He felt he could keep them quiet if he stayed there, but otherwise there might be lawsuits and attachments. It's unclear whether the Flint investors were told this before the sale was complete.

They were certain, however, they needed David's services. So they endorsed a note for his debts, a local bank provided the money and David began work in Flint. The bank reasonably insisted, though, that David not receive his stock until his debts had been paid out of its dividends. Briscoe figured rightly that this would never happen – the dividends would never catch up with the debt. But Briscoe wrote: "It can be said, however, that as the stock developed its real value, that those who finally secured it gave Mr. Buick a considerable sum of money, although legally not obliged to do so." Carl Crow, in the book *The City of Flint Grows Up,* said the note was eventually paid off but not from earnings of the Buick company.

Reminiscing from the perspective of 1921, Briscoe wrote that with Buick's move to Flint, "thus began that great era in the life of that quiet and pretty town, a town which has produced, it is said, more millionaires than any other place since Cortez discovered the golden temples of Mexico."

Now that Buick had financial backing and a new factory, it was time to fulfill Whiting's "broader opportunity." After more than five years of working with engines and automobiles in this volatile period, David knew where to go to revisit the idea of Buick Motor Company building automobiles.

Chapter 10

First Flint Buick

On January 8, 1904, David Buick wrote to "friend Marr" that he had heard Marr had just quit another company – Reid Manufacturing, where he worked briefly on its Wolverine touring car.

Walter Marr had moved from company to company after leaving Buick Auto-Vim and Power Company in March of 1901. As described earlier, he built a few curved-dash Oldsmobiles in Detroit in the spring of '01, perfected a bicycle engine for a Detroit firm that summer, spent six months (August 1901-February 1902) in Cleveland with the American Motor Carriage Company, worked briefly at Buick Manufacturing Company in the late winter or early spring of 1902 and then concentrated during much of 1902 and 1903 on developing the Marr Autocar.

His latest assignment, with Reid, started December 1, 1903, and ended barely a month later, on January 5, 1904. No reason was given for the quick departure, which seems puzzling as Reid's Wolverine was about to get an engine built by Buick, a firm Marr knew well. Perhaps his stint at Reid was intended as a short assignment. The firm did assure him in a letter: "Beg to advise, that work which you have done is satisfactory. If we can be of any assistance to you in getting another position, we will be very glad to do so."

Therefore, in early 1904, Marr was ripe for a new assignment. News of his departure from Reid traveled fast – Buick's letter to Marr was written only three days later. In his letter, David Buick asked Marr to phone or visit him at his Detroit home. While Buick spent the workweek in Flint, he lived in his family home on Meldrum in Detroit on weekends. Marr and Buick had a cordial visit there one day. They immediately agreed to work together again.

But Marr made a specific demand. Maybe he had begun to re-

103

flect on difficult relationships over the last few years, not only arguments with David Buick but also incidents and disagreements at Oldsmobile, American Motor Carriage, Marr Autocar and possibly Reid Manufacturing. It was time to take a gentler tack.

He told David they must have an enlightened relationship: "I come back with this understanding, Mr. Buick – If I'm hot I'll wait till I cool off to talk; if you're hot, you wait till you've cooled off." Or, as Marr told Charles Hulse, he wanted both to agree that in any dispute they would wait until the next day "when reasoning power has returned to both." By April of 1904, Marr was working with David Buick in Flint (and he would remain at the Buick firm into retirement, and beyond). And, no surprise, by the first week in June, 1904, a new Buick automobile was being driven around the company's yards.

Marr's story is he persuaded Whiting to build automobiles. Whiting was at first disinterested, but agreed to think about it if Marr could drive a car to Detroit and back, touching certain points along the way. While Whiting likely wanted to build an automobile from Day One, he was cautious as a businessman. He may also have feigned reluctance so the other directors would believe he was being prudent and conservative.

It's not clear how much help Buick and Marr had. Arthur W. Hough, who claimed in published articles to have built six automobiles in Perry, Mich., between 1900 and 1906, said Buick and Marr were experimenting in Detroit when they heard of the Hough cars. Hough said he used a one-cylinder Buick engine he obtained from David Buick in Detroit for an automobile he built in 1903. In his fifth and sixth cars, built in 1905 and 1906, he used the Buick Model B two-cylinder engines "because they had a lot of power to get up and go." (Hough was also said to have been a test driver for A.B.C. Hardy's Flint roadsters).

According to Hough, Buick and Marr asked him to come to Detroit. But by the time he was ready to drive his car there, he received word to go to Flint instead – Buick and Marr had moved there. Hough sold one of his cars to Buick Motor Company and in May of 1905

David Buick talked him into taking a job in Buick's experimental department in Jackson. He worked at Buick until his retirement in 1946 at age 82.

On one of his first visits to Flint after selling his car to Buick, Hough said he saw it parked at a hitching post on Saginaw Street, the city's main street. He found the owner in a store and asked how the car was working. The man, who had bought it from Buick, said it performed flawlessly and wondered: "Why do you ask?" Hough replied: "Oh, I just built it, that's all. And I was wondering if it was standing up."

Hough's influence, if any, on the earliest Buicks is unknown. But some details on building the first Flint Buick are recorded. Bert Calver, a Flint Wagon Works assembler, remembered both the excitement and the difficulty of building it. "All of us were pretty excited to be working on the very first (Flint) Buick," he told Ben Bennett of the *Flint News-Advertiser* in 1953.

"They just came in and told us one day that we were going to work on the Buick. They gave us some blueprints to go by but a lot of the design had to be made up as went along."

First, wagon works craftsmen created a body of wood. (Later, the W. F. Stewart Company made the bodies and the Flint Wagon Works upholstered and painted them.) Then they built the frame and chassis from huge angle irons. Springs and axles were brought from Armstrong Spring and Axle Company across town. They were hauled over in Bert Armstrong's 1902 curved-dash Oldsmobile, remembered James Parkhill, Armstrong's successor as the firm's president.

"Whenever we got stuck," said Calver, "we just did things the way we had done them with buggies. Sounds funny to say that we lined up the wheels with an old pine yardstick and the frame with a piece of string, but that's the way we did it – same as we'd lined up thousands of buggies.

"There was no such thing as welding, so all the parts had to be joined with rivets. And none of the bolts we used were cut to size. We just went to the barrel and hunted around for bolts we thought might fit. And if they were too long, we just cut them off."

David Buick (left) and Walter Marr at work at Buick Motor Company, a rare candid photo.

The engine was too large for the frame so workers hacked at the angle irons with cold chisels for hours to make room. Then they carried the frame and motor to the Buick plant. "It was just across the street," Calver said. "But it was a job."

William Beacraft's notes said the engine was ready for the car on May 27, 1904. On June 4, *The Wolverine Citizen* reported "the first automobile to be made by the Buick Motor Works was finished this week."

First Flint Buick

On January 8, 1904, David Buick is ready to invite Walter Marr back to Buick.

But even as this first Flint Buick car was being conceived and created, the Buick Model B engine, already in production, was earning a reputation for power. Companies building the Dolson car in Charlotte, Mich., the Jackson in Jackson, Mich., and the Sommer and Wayne in Detroit contracted with Buick to provide engines though it's unknown when they actually bought and installed them.

Individuals also took advantage of the opportunity to trade up to a Buick engine. Charles Hulse pointed out Flint's automobile culture had not been waiting on Buick. By the spring of 1903, some of Flint's wealthy young men, such as carriage maker William Paterson's son, Will, and William C. Orrell, a cousin of Billy Durant, were buying red Wintons and causing such a nuisance with their noise frightening horses that local citizens called them the "Red Devils." Even Durant, noting his cousin had an automobile, huffed about the "noisy contraptions" and said he was "mighty provoked with anyone who would drive around annoying people that way."

About a month after young Paterson bought a Winton in April 1903, four new 1903 Thomas touring cars, all painted bright red, arrived in Flint by train for local citizens William Wildanger, Francis Flanders, George V. Cotharin and Harry W. Watson. The "Red Devils" were growing in numbers as well as notoriety.

By July of 1904, Cotharin had concluded his Thomas's one-cylinder engine was so weak "it wouldn't pull a hen off a nest," as Roger Van Bolt, director of Sloan Museum, once related. Cotharin took the car to the Buick plant and had the engine replaced with a new two-cylinder Buick Model B engine. In 1909 apparently this same car showed up in the St. Louis, Mo., railroad station, serving as a photographer's prop for years. Its 1904 pushrods-on-bottom Buick engine is one of the two survivors from that year, today the centerpiece of a Model B Buick car created with a complete body. (Thomas engines later got better. In 1908, a Thomas Flyer won the famous New York-to-Paris "Great Race").

For a time, David Buick was the company's spokesman with the press. On May 21, 1904, he told the *Flint Daily News* the company was employing a day shift of 90 men and a night force of 50. "This has been a banner week since we began operations," Buick said. "We turned out 22 completed engines this week and have more orders than we can fill."

On June 18, he complained to the same paper about being overworked. "I miss my half holiday on Saturdays since I came to Flint," Buick said. "When I was in Detroit, our factory, the Buick & Sherwood plant, never operated on Saturday afternoons. I am a great believer in the Saturday half holiday, and would like to see it adapted by the manufacturers in Flint."

Whiting and the Flint Wagon Works directors might well have been puzzled to see that quote in the newspaper from the Buick company's leader.

On Saturday, July 9, the first Flint Buick automobile was ready

First Flint Buick

Arthur W. Hough: Early car builder worked at Buick from 1906 to 1946.

for its big test. It didn't look ready, lacking body and fenders. "One of the new Buick autos was on the streets this afternoon and attracted considerable favorable attention," *The Flint Journal* reported. "The machine was not wholly completed but from its speed it looks as though the Buick will cut quite a figure in the auto world when the company gets to turning them out in greater numbers."

Walter Marr and Buick's son, Tom, were aboard, wearing dusters and caps and goggles. About 1:15 p.m., they left the Bryant House hotel in downtown Flint, with Marr driving, and headed south on a 90-mile test drive to Detroit via Lapeer. A rear bearing failed near Lapeer, so they stayed the night there and fixed the bearing. They

David Buick's Marvelous Motor Car

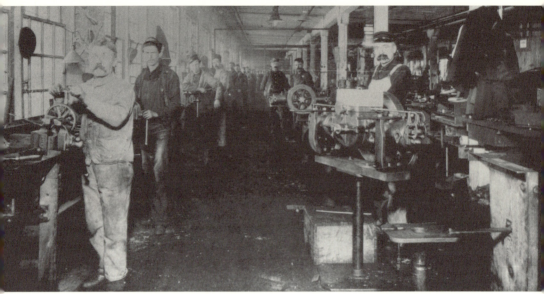

Photo in the Buick factory on W. Kearsley Street in Flint in late 1904 documents transition from pushrods-on-bottom Model B engine to pushrods-on-top Model C engine. William Beacraft, engine plant foreman and master mechanic, is at right with the new engine while the nearest man behind him, named Randall, has the earlier version. Others in the photo (from left) are Morse, reaming a taper-pin hole for the cams; Hiles; Wascher; Daikin; and then 11 unidentified workers. A man named Green is third from right.

arrived in Detroit at noon the next day, Sunday, July 10, "covered with mud and grime," according to Hulse. Since both men were from Detroit, they spent the day visiting relatives and friends. While Marr visited several local auto plants and took notes on Monday, Tom Buick went to city hall and paid $1 to buy car license No. 1024. They headed back to Flint Tuesday.

This ride of July 12, 1904, would be remembered in the annals of Buick. A steady rain deepened the mud in the roads, but the car ran well, averaging 30 miles per hour. "I did the driving and Buick was kept busy wiping the mud off my goggles," said Marr. When an electric car showed up to challenge them in one town, the Buick "showed them the way," Marr said. In another town, "we went so fast…we could not see the village six-mile-an-hour sign," he said. Had he been ticketed? The question was not asked or answered.

First Flint Buick

"At one place, going down a hill, I saw a bump at a bridge too late to slow up. When I hit it, I threw on all the power and landed over it safely in the road. Buick was just taking a chew of tobacco, and a lump of mud as large as a baseball hit him square in the face, filling his mouth completely. We were plastered with mud from head to foot when we reached Flint."

The route was 115 miles instead of about 90, because Marr missed a turn at Lapeer. They covered it in 217 minutes. Marr declared that was a record. Marr drove directly to the office of *The Flint Journal* and told a reporter: "The machine made the run without a skip. It reached here in the best of condition. We took the hills handily with our high-speed gear and the machine sounded like a locomotive. It simply climbed."

The impressed reporter, noting Marr's words and the mud-caked appearance of the men and car, tapped out this lead: "Bespattered with flying real estate from every county they had touched, but with the knowledge that they had made a 'record,' Tom Buick and W.L. Marr, of the Buick Motor Works, who left for Detroit on Saturday to give the first automobile turned out by that concern a trial on the road, returned to the city late yesterday afternoon. The test of the machine was eminently satisfactory, and, in fact, exceeded expectations."

The two men posed in the Buick for a memorable photo by professional photographer Charles Quay on E. First Street between Saginaw Street and Brush Alley downtown, almost in front of *The Journal* office, and then for another on the mud-rutted roadway at the one-story brick factory. (Quay, writing to Charles Hulse in 1956, said he had known the Buick family since its Buick & Sherwood days in Detroit and also had taken photos of Flint Wagon Works and Durant-Dort vehicles for those firms. "Tom Buick and I used to go out together to photograph the Buick climbing hills," he recalled.)

Upon their return from Detroit, the two found Whiting and his associates waiting with the decision David Buick and Marr had wanted. When Marr told the little group, "We're here," they responded, "So are we," meaning they would finance the beginning of automobile production. The Buick would go to market.

In the best known of all Buick historical photos, Walter Marr (above) drives the first Flint Buick back into Flint July 12, 1904, after making a test run to Detroit. David Buick's son Tom (above right) joined him on the round trip. The photo was taken on E. First Street near Brush Alley. The Flint Journal *office is in the background at right. Later in the day (below), Marr, Tom Buick and the same car are at the new Buick factory on W. Kearsley.*

First Flint Buick

Hulse interviewed Marr in 1934 and asked him why the road test was necessary. Marr replied:

> When I came to Flint in April of 1904, and joined the Buick company, their main line of business was the building of stationary gasoline engines. Mr. Whiting, who had the 'say-so' in the company, carried the thinking that the money was to be made in the engine business. He thought so many firms had got into the automobile business that the market would soon be saturated with cars.
>
> I told Whiting that my interest was in the building of automobiles and that we could make a successful car at the Buick. After several approaches to Whiting on this subject, he finally relented and told me that if I could build up a sample model and prove that it had good possibilities then he would reconsider the idea of Buick building automobiles. After our successful road test run to Detroit, Mr. Whiting gave the go-ahead to build up a few cars to see how they would sell.

Like a number of other auto pioneers, David Buick boasted of his vision of the future of the automobile. He probably wrote the biographical sketch in 1913 that noted in a discussion with officers of his company in 1903 or early 1904 "he declared with enthusiasm that the end of twenty years would find only the surface of the business scratched – that in time horse-drawn vehicles would be little more than reminders of a past age. In his mind's eye he could see the immense traffic of the automobile as it is known today...."

More photos were taken later in the summer of the first production Buick automobile alongside the one-story brick Buick factory. These were hardly glamour shots. The car sits in a rutted yard or road with bits of wood and other debris visibly sticking out of the mud. Bicycles are leaning against the factory wall, a man is peering out a plant window and a woman is watching the photographer from the factory porch. Several telephone poles complete the image.

There is one of the car alone, with a sign propped against the running board ("Buick Motor Co., Flint, Mich."). There is one with Marr

License form signed in Detroit by Tom Buick on July 11, 1904, during the test run.

at the wheel, alone in the car. And still another with the dignitaries – Marr and Tom Buick in the front seat, James Whiting and Buick's new president, Charles M. Begole, in the back.

An opportunity was missed for a truly historical photo. Why wasn't David Buick in that photo instead of his son? Wasn't he in Flint that day? Did he ask for his son to be in the photo instead of himself? The odd fact is, there is no known photo of David Buick with a Buick automobile.

As for the first Flint Buicks, Marr is seen as the expert in putting together an entire automobile correctly. But Hugh Dolnar, who in 1904 wrote the first Buick test-ride report, credited David Buick for the body. David, he wrote, "conceived the happy idea of hinging the side entrance doors in front. This gives two distinct advantages, first, a good substantial door hinge, and second, in connection with the full-length running board, the swinging of the door to the front gives the easiest possible entrance to the tonneau seats." No suicide doors for Buick.

Marr and his engine superintendent were so confident in the Model B that he and Mason each drove one to the track at Grosse Pointe, Mich., on August 27, 1904. For the first time ever, Buicks were in a

First Flint Buick

First Buick Model B in the summer of 1904, with the Flint Buick factory in the background. From left, front seat, are Walter Marr and Tom Buick. From left, rear seat, are Charles Begole and, in a straw hat, James Whiting. Whiting brought Buick to Flint in 1903 and Begole became Buick president later in 1904.

race. Marr finished third behind Frank Kulick in the famous Ford 999 and W. F. Winchester in a Franklin. Mason was fourth. Not an overly impressive start, perhaps, but the Buick would soon do much better. (David Buick skipped the race, instead taking his wife and younger son Wynton on a weekend holiday). Also that month, David told reporters the original business had grown so much that two stories and a test shed would be added to the one-story factory, which happened in 1905. An ad in *The Implement Age* of September 22, 1904, said the plant was capable of turning out 2,600 engines per year and "we want agents in every town." There was optimism everywhere.

Dr. Herbert H. Hills, first buyer of a Flint production Buick, with his car. In September of 1904, Hills would use it to give Billy Durant his first ride in a Buick.

The first Flint Buick to be sold was bought by a 23-year-old Flint physician, Herbert H. Hills. The son of a lumberman from nearby Davison, he bought it for $500 on July 27, 1904, per Dolnar, or August 13, per Hills' diary. As Dolnar noted, Hills had driven it day and night continually without incident up until September 16, when Dolnar arrived at Flint, "and believes he has the best car in the world."

Actually, Hills remembered there were a few problems. He carried a hairpin when driving so he could quickly clean the spark plugs. "There was something wrong with the piston rings, they couldn't keep soot from getting out of the cylinder and covering the plugs," he

1905 Model C Buick, the official factory photo.

recalled in a 1953 interview with the *Flint News-Advertiser.*

And once, when he couldn't start the car for an early morning trip, he ran to the railroad station, caught a horse taxi to Walter Marr's house on E. Kearsley Street and called until Marr woke up. As Hills recalled, Marr "leaned out the window and said, 'Hello, doc. What's the trouble?' I told him the car had stopped and he said to give him time to put on pants and a shirt and he'd be right down." Hills took the interurban to his destination, and Marr took the car. It was discovered water had gotten into the gasoline. "It probably isn't as common these days to wake up the chief engineer of Buick to fix your car," Hills commented in 1953.

The doctor was also impressed by the car's light weight. "I could lift the rear end by myself," he said. "That certainly came in handy changing tires. I'd just lift up the rear end and slide the jack in underneath."

Dolnar reported Hills' car was the July 9-12 test car now completed with full body and fenders. But the *Flint Daily News* on July

29, 1904, said the car "that made the fast run to Detroit and back three weeks ago" had been shipped to Chicago the previous day. And years later Marr said that on a visit to Chicago in the 1920s, he saw that Buick's engine being used to pump water.

The company turned out 16 Buicks, Model Bs, in the summer of 1904 by the time Dolnar (pen name for Horace Arnold), writing for *Cycle and Automobile Trade Journal,* arrived in town. Orders for 11 more were on the books. Dolnar was given his test ride the following morning, September 17. This car was a newly built model, not yet test driven.

Tom Buick took the wheel, and Dolnar took notes: "At first, Buick drove with some decent regard for law and prudence. But the road was hard, the clear air was intoxicating, and after one request to 'push her' up one steep hill, which the car mounted at 25 miles speed, Buick began to be proud of his mount and drive for fun…The car simply ran to perfection…the car flew down the hills and flew up the hills, all the same rate, and the engine purred and the wind whistled past and the soft September sun smiled benignly on the fine farms we ran by, and it was all delightful." Even though a policeman stopped Buick, fined him $12 for fast driving, and told him it would be more next time.

The drive was obviously a critical success. Dolnar found the Buick car "thoroughly responsive; had more power everywhere than could be used."

A statement in Dolnar's article that the Buick generated more than 20 horsepower was "very generally questioned," he wrote in a later issue. So he ran more tests and concluded "the power of the Buick motor was not less than first stated…and can give about 29 brake horse power at 1320 crank-shaft turns per minute." Chiding his critics, he continued that his account "should be accepted as showing that those reputable gas-engine builders who assert that not more than 16 B.H. P. can be had from a pair of 4 1/2x5 opposed cylinders are more familiar with their own motors than with the Buick model under test, and that while the writer is, unfortunately, compelled to do work in haste, he is not wrong in the stories he tells."

Walter Marr (left) and David Buick: Another rare candid photo of the two at work together.

In its 1905 catalog, Buick made much of the notion Dolnar's original report had "startled the whole mechanical world." In October 1904, Buick's first automobile ad stated: "In a class by itself. Actual 21 Brake Horse Power on the stand. Experienced drivers can get the same on the road."

Hugh Dolnar's words of September 17, 1904, would have been a fine birthday present for David Buick, who turned 50 that very day (though the review didn't show up until the October issue). But despite the great publicity of that review, reality had dawned on James Whiting: Starting an automobile manufacturing operation chewed up huge amounts of money compared with the carriage industry. Also, he had discovered, David Buick was no business leader. The directors had invested $37,500 during the startup, and the company had not only exhausted that but owed $25,000 each to three Flint banks. Even the stationary engines, for which Buick salesmen had received large orders, were not being produced fast enough.

On the surface, Buick Motor Company looked as if it were on the brink of success. But that was far from true. In fact, Whiting once admitted, it was insolvent. He figured it needed two things – a younger man to run the business and more money.

Whiting, the story goes, was bound by train for a carriage convention in Chicago when he discussed his problems with Fred A. Aldrich, secretary of Flint's largest carriage firm, the Durant-Dort Carriage

David Buick's Marvelous Motor Car

Company. Both were sure they knew the right man for the job of saving Buick – but he was a man preoccupied by the stock market in New York. And he didn't like automobiles much. But he was a booster of Flint, and he had a lot of friends and relatives whose finances were tied up in those Flint banks. It was time to talk to Billy Durant.

Chapter 11

The irrepressible Billy Durant

As he studied his options for financial help, James H. Whiting decided he would have no problem reaching out to a competitor. After all, by 1904 William C. Durant was already a magical name in Flint. Grandson of a Michigan governor of the Civil War era, Henry Howland Crapo, Durant was a latecomer to Flint's carriage industry, but he quickly surpassed them all.

On a September evening in 1886, the young businessman hitched a ride in friend Johnny Alger's horse-drawn road cart in downtown Flint. Captivated with the way its patented spring suspension cushioned the bumps, he immediately took a train to Coldwater, Mich., where the cart was manufactured, and bought the rights to build it.

Durant was a very personable young man, about 5-foot-8, slim and often flashing a dazzling smile. He moved quickly and, as a 1931 voice recording reveals, spoke with a clipped Boston accent, a holdover from his childhood. Durant had been about 10 when he moved with his family from Boston to Flint. His actions and speech radiated energy and confidence. He was a natural salesman, trying his hand at patent medicine, cigars and insurance, while running the Flint Water Works on the side.

In 1886, when he needed money to close the deal with the Coldwater Road Cart Company, he avoided banks where his family had influence because "if I make a failure of the venture, I will never hear the end of it." So he went to another bank, Citizens National, where he had no problem persuading its president, Robert J. Whaley, to loan him $2,000 on a 90-day renewable note.

Durant quickly found a partner – friend Josiah Dallas Dort, who put in $1,000 he borrowed from his mother. (In Whaley's restored home in Flint, the original Citizens National bank book of the Flint Road Cart

David Buick's Marvelous Motor Car

William C. (Billy) Durant, probably photographed during 1906 Glidden Tour

Company is displayed, with the first entries of September 28, 1886, being deposits of $1,000 each by Durant and Dort – the first document in a series of events that led to the creation of General Motors).*

---

* While Durant would always be the promotional genius of their carriage businesses and then their early automobile ventures, Dallas Dort was his anchor – the leader who handled the overall job and details of managing the financial and manufacturing operations, including labor and Flint civic duties. As Arthur Pound once quoted Durant's lawyer, John J. Carton: "Billy never thought that GM would become the big manufacturer it did. What he desired, most of all, were large stock issues in which he, from an inside position, could dicker and trade. After Billy left Durant-Dort for Buick there were always too many yes men around him for his own good. Dallas Dort and Charlie Nash and Fred Aldrich and the rest of them in Durant-Dort could bring Billy down to earth. Away from them he just soared, high, wide and handsome."

The irrepressible Billy Durant

One of the first 16 Model Bs of 1904 on the road, here with William Beacraft, Buick engine production foreman, and his family. Beacraft bought it in 1907 from E. E. Edwards, a Flint wholesale grocer, the second person in Flint to buy a Buick.

Then he shipped his only existing road cart to a big fair in Wisconsin, and began to work. To Durant, the road cart was a "self-seller," and he was confident nobody could match him in selling a genuinely appealing product. His self-confidence was not misplaced. Even though his sample road cart showed up very late at the fair, Durant took orders for an astonishing 600 carts before he had built one. He went home to Flint and contracted with the best local carriage maker, William A. Paterson, to build 1,200 carts at $12.50 each. He figured he could sell them for nearly twice that.

By the turn of the century his Flint Road Cart Company, renamed in 1895 as the Durant-Dort Carriage Company, was said to be the leading volume producer of horse-drawn vehicles in the United States. Durant had pulled together suppliers from across the country and had created what automotive historians would someday label "the General Motors of the carriage era." It was a giant concern and Dallas Dort called Durant "easily our leading force and genius."

David Buick's Marvelous Motor Car

A.B.C. Hardy (left), Flint's first car manufacturer, with W.C. Durant and wife Catherine.

In 1904, Durant, though only 42, was semi-retired from the carriage industry and playing the stock market in New York. Like most carriage leaders, he was no fan of automobiles. A.B.C. Hardy, who had been president of the Durant-Dort Carriage Company before building Hardy Flint roadsters, remembered going to a carriage convention in New York along with about 350 other participants, including fellow Flintites Whiting, Durant and Dort. They were all offered an opportunity to take a side trip to ride in a horseless carriage. Hardy said only he and Whiting jumped at the chance "to see and ride in those strange contraptions." When he asked Durant why he didn't try

The irrepressible Billy Durant

Billy Durant (left) and Dallas Dort talk outside Buick headquarters in Flint, with Imperial Wheel in background. The building below is the Durant-Dort Carriage Company headquarters in Flint. It is now a National Historic Landmark, its offices tied to the birth of General Motors.

them out, Durant said banker friends had told him automobiles "were to be sold to rich men for their foolish sons, and that some doctors were buying them."

Hardy went to Europe, learned of the bustling automobile industry there, and came back to Durant with a warning he should get out of the horse-drawn vehicle business. "Billy, there is something coming that will sweep it away," Hardy said. "Get into this horseless carriage field...."

Durant, always polite and patient, listened carefully, and then said: "We have more business than we can handle. Ours is a permanent business, and we are going to add another factory."

But enthusiasm for automobiles was beginning to take off, even in the carriage capital of Flint, and even among relatives of the carriage king. Arthur Jerome Eddy, who had grown up in Flint and married Durant's cousin, Lucy Crapo Orrell, was a Chicago lawyer when in 1901 he wrote a book, *Two Thousand Miles on an Automobile,* using only the pen name "Chauffeur." It was an account of his incredible long-distance trip in an unidentified car (it was a one-cylinder, 8 ½-horsepower Winton). Eddy drove out of Chicago on August 1, 1901, and on to Boston, New York City and Albany. He then returned through Canada to Sarnia, Ontario, and on to Flint to visit his parents. The roads, he reported, were best in Canada, worst in Michigan. He then drove to Montreal and had the car shipped back to Chicago. For 1901 it was a stunning adventure, said to be the longest auto trip yet taken in the United States.

Eddy's conclusion: "Any woman can drive an electric automobile, any man can drive a steam; but neither man nor woman can drive a gasoline; it follows its own odorous will and goes or goes not as it feels disposed."

In 1902, Eddy, by then the owner of a Panhard and visiting his parents again, gave rides to a number of Flint citizens, notably Dallas Dort. Durant's daughter Margery also got a ride in the car. When she raced into the house to tell her father of her exciting adventure, Durant scolded her for taking a foolish chance.

Clearly, the prospect of selling an automobile concern to Durant

Buick factory on W. Kearsley after being expanded from one to three stories.

would be daunting for Whiting. But if he wanted to save Buick Motor Company, he needed to be persuasive with his case. Durant was not only a great salesman but he also had no peer as an organizer and promoter. And with his connections, he could put Wall Street money behind a product. As Fred Aldrich, the Durant-Dort secretary, remembered, he advised Whiting: "William C. Durant is the man who can put Buick on its feet." Whiting, working through Aldrich and Durant's partner, Dallas Dort, asked him to come home and take a look at Buick.

So Durant returned to Flint in the fall of 1904. Although he was admittedly dubious about automobiles, he was loyal to Flint and liked a good business challenge. Possibly more important, he was concerned Flint banks, where he and his many relatives and friends did business and had ownership, were being made vulnerable by their loans to Buick. And so he would check out the Buick proposition.

Dr. Herbert H. Hills gave Durant his first ride in a Buick on September 4, 1904, per Hills' diary. It's a story remembered by Hills himself in an interview shortly before his death in 1953. "We started off with Durant and me in the front seat, and Mrs. Durant and their daughter in the rear. We drove out East Kearsley Street, then one of the few paved streets in Flint, and Durant kept firing questions at me

Durant lines up every Buick available at Saginaw and First streets in downtown Flint November 3, 1904 – his first publicity event after taking control two days earlier.

about how the car ran and if I liked it or not. We didn't talk about anything else the whole time." (Hills joined Buick as assistant sales manager in 1906 and left Buick for Packard in 1909).

As Donald E. Johnson, husband of Whiting's granddaughter, Alice, told the writer in the 1970s, Whiting then drove Durant around Flint, and they pulled up in front of Whiting's house and talked for an hour. When Whiting walked into his house, he told his family: "Billy's sold!"

Sam McLaughlin, longtime chairman of GM of Canada, told several versions of a different story. In his recollections, Durant revealed no intent to study the Buick proposition when he arrived back in Flint in the fall of 1904. McLaughlin said Marr drove one of the first Buicks to Durant's office, but Durant refused to ride in it. "Then

later, Walter and Dave Buick drove it up and down past Mr. Durant's house all that evening, and then the next day induced Mr. Durant to go out in it for a ride."

Although the elderly McLaughlin, recalling this story to Buick General Manager Ed Rollert in a 1964 letter, wrongly remembered Marr came from Lansing with the car, he had known Durant from the carriage era and presented the anecdote as a well-known fact. He had provided more detail to Eric Hutton in *MacLean's* magazine 10 years earlier, relating that after Durant refused to even look at the car, Marr taught Dallas Dort how to drive it.

Dort returned to the office and said excitedly to Durant: "Come on out! It's great. They taught me how to drive. I've been driving a car!" To which Durant replied, "I want nothing to do with it."

But Marr kept driving the car back and forth in front of Durant's house, that evening and then the next morning (along with David

Buick, according to McLaughlin's letter to Rollert). Durant, finally impressed with Marr's persistence if not the car, agreed to go for a ride. According to McLaughlin, Durant then learned Marr was not trying to sell him a Buick car, but the Buick company!

All of this could be at least partially true, starting with Durant's first ride with Hills, coaxed into a second ride by Marr and Buick, and the clincher meeting with Whiting (though McLaughlin's memory, like Durant's, was at least occasionally more creative than entirely accurate).

There are also oft-repeated accounts of Durant taking the Buick out himself, test driving it around Flint. Durant put the Buick "through swamps, mud and sand and pitchholes for almost two months," wrote Arthur Pound in *The Turning Wheel*. Others are doubtful, characterizing Durant as a super salesman, super promoter and super organizer of big business, but no test driver.

But he should have driven the car and probably did. He was about to make an important decision. The master salesman needed to persuade himself this was indeed a great product. The roads around Flint were poor but the Buick engine was always up to the challenge. Durant became convinced. This car performed.

Dort once said Durant would have gotten into automobiles sooner or later because he was a gambler – he would have been in the thick of the California gold rush, or in railroads, in earlier times. Perhaps, but he certainly wouldn't have chosen such an unlikely enterprise as Buick had he not been persuaded by his friends and relatives in his adopted home town of Flint.

Now that he was enthusiastic about the product, Durant needed to find out how serious the stockholders were about placing the business on a sound financial footing. There was money in Flint – fortunes had been made in lumbering, carriages and even cigar-making. But it now needed to be invested in the new business in town. Buick was important to the city's economy and it could not survive undercapitalized and heavily in debt.

Durant said his investigation of the firm in the fall of 1904 "ascertained that it was practically insolvent," agreeing with Whiting's

1905 Model C with William C. Durant's daughter Margery. This was the first model Buick to combine the expertise of David Buick, Walter Marr and W.C. Durant.

assessment. However, he said in a 1911 legal document, he believed that if the business were "properly conducted and vigorously prosecuted, there was a fair prospect of bettering such condition."

Under Durant's prodding, Buick's stockholders agreed to increase the capital stock to $300,000 on November 1, 1904, and to raise it again to $500,000 on November 19. Of this, $175,000 would go to the stockholders and the remaining $325,000 would be turned over to Durant "as his sole individual property to be used by him in his sole judgment he deemed for the best interest of said company...," according to the legal document. Coincidentally (or maybe not), at virtually the same time, owners of the Flint Gas Light Company sold that firm to other interests for $325,000 and it is reported Durant persuaded the sellers to invest much of that money in Buick stock.

With the financial details agreed upon, finally the decision was made. On November 1, 1904, Durant was elected to the Buick board. He was now in charge but declined the presidency in favor of Charles Begole, a Flint Wagon Works director and son of a former Michigan governor, Josiah Begole. Whiting resigned to devote more time to the wagon works, but he would soon be working with Durant again.

General Motors celebrates its birth date as September 16, 1908, when the company was incorporated – but the real beginning of GM was November 1, 1904, when Billy Durant took control of Buick. This was the spark. Once Durant held control of Buick and properly capitalized the company, the great success story was launched.

The decision of the stockholders to agree to Durant's proposal is both a tribute to his reputation and a sign of how desperate they were to keep the company solvent. Their money and their trust were well placed. Durant quickly turned Buick around and made each share of stock a fabulous investment. The decision also quickened David Buick's long slide from power and influence.

As an immediate example of his showmanship, Durant created a Buick event on November 3, 1904, two days after taking control. He paraded eight Buicks – all he could find and several not yet completed – through downtown Flint "with tooting bugles…(creating) a great deal of attention and much favorable comment," *The Flint Daily News* reported. Another historic photo bearing Charles Quay's imprint captures the Buicks lined up at Saginaw and First streets, one of the city's main intersections.

Durant avoided one sticky problem by quietly obtaining a license late in the year so Buick could join the Association of Licensed Automobile Manufacturers. This was the organization that tried to control the industry under the patent of George B. Selden. The ALAM was blamed by A.B.C. Hardy for forcing his Flint Automobile Company out of business in 1903. Durant realized he would have to deal with the ALAM so he bought the failing Pope-Robinson Company and obtained its license. The ALAM's control was eventually ended thanks to the legal fight of Henry Ford, to the general relief of the industry as a whole.

Buick produced only 37 cars in 1904 (forget the incorrect old

Design for early Buick catalog covers (above). Early ad for two-cylinder valve-in-head engine (above right). First Buick automobile ad, in Cycle and Automobile Trade Journal, *October 1904 (right). Model B ads in same publication in November (below left) and December (below right) of 1904. Note the only major change in the illustration is the wider brass molding over the radiator in December.*

accounts that 16 were made in 1903; the first 16 were made between June 1904 and September 16, 1904). With Billy Durant aboard, the small number was meaningless. After all, local people still talked about how he had started in road carts, purchasing one cart and shipping it to a Wisconsin fair. There, he talked the judges into giving him a blue ribbon. He then took 600 orders for his "Famous Blue Ribbon Line" of carts before he had even figured out how to build them.*

With Buick, he followed the same pattern. With fewer than 40 Buicks under the company's belt, Durant shipped a car and a chassis to the New York Auto Show of January 1905 and within a few days had accepted orders for 1,108 Buicks. As his wife Clara wrote to a friend: "The Buick certainly is a success." To Durant, the Buick, like his first road cart, was a "self seller" – a product so good it could sell itself. David Buick and Walter Marr had produced an automobile that was not only mechanically and cosmetically pleasing, but could navigate mud and steep hills like no other automobile he had ever seen.

Just as Durant had done with the road cart, he had backed a vehicle with a unique attribute (spring suspension with the road cart, overhead-valve engine with the Buick), emphasized the asset and made a large number of sales, largely because of his own engaging

---

* Production numbers for Buick in 1903, 1904 and 1905 have often been confused. Here is the writer's version: Beyond the one experimental Buick built in Detroit by Walter Marr (1899-1901) and the second built in Detroit by David Buick for Ben Briscoe (1902-03), the first group of Buicks were 16 1904 Model Bs – the first production Buicks – built in Flint between early June and September 16, 1904, all but one built after mid July. No Buick was ever advertised as a 1904 model, but those cars were clearly 1904s. Among the 16 was the July 9-12 test car, later fitted with a body and sold. By the end of calendar 1904, 37 Buicks had been built, including those 16. At least some of the last 21 cars built in 1904 were advertised in the first Buick car ads as the 1905 Model B. In 1905, Buick built in Jackson, Mich., 750 Model Cs according to official records, but only 729 according to William Gregor, a later owner of a Model C who saw the official records before they disappeared. But if the 21 from late 1904 (assuming they are assigned as 1905 models) are added to the 729, the total is 750. According to official records, there was no 1905 Model B, but clearly such a model was advertised and presumably sold late in 1904. The designation was changed so quickly from Model B to Model C that the total may have just been folded into 1905 Model C production. It's also possible the number 750 was created merely by rounding off the numbers built in Jackson in 1905.

Dealer drive-away of Model C Buicks in downtown Jackson in 1905 (below).

personality and relentless energy.

Durant immediately promoted engine performance. The company noted in a catalog, "the first conspicuous event that impressed the general public…was furnished on Thanksgiving Day (November 24, 1904) at Eagle Rock near Newark, New Jersey. That day marked America's greatest and severest hill-climbing contest."

The Motor World told the story: "In the class for cars between $850 and $1,250, the new Buick car made its initial appearance, and in a twinkling stamped itself as a wonder. It easily carried off the first honors in its class by a wide margin…the clean-cut and businesslike appearance of the car and its quiet running caused much favorable comment."

The Buick company pointed out the car was "not specially built or geared for hill climbing or for racing; it was a regular stock model" and driven by "a gentleman (dealer H. J. Koehler) who is in no sense a professional" whereas many of its competitors "were specially built or specially geared and driven by factory experts."

David Buick's Marvelous Motor Car

Durant took David Buick with him to the New York show, and it became apparent other automobile writers had been reading about the Buick engine. The overhead-valve engine was news in New York.

The Motor World reported in its discussion of the show: "There is one newcomer which must command the attention of the public, the Buick, already famous for claims of wonderful development of horsepower from a relatively small engine...Twenty-two guaranteed horsepower from two 4 ½ by 5 cylinders is equal to, if not in excess of, the best performances by a motor of any kind."

The publication also interviewed the reticent David Buick. It reported: "Mr. Buick...very generally and in a very nice way explains why he is certainly getting more horsepower than engines of similar size." It followed with this explanation:

> In the first place his valves, 1 7/8 inches in diameter, are at the end of the cylinder; the diameter given is generous. The gas as it enters, enters the piston clearance at the end of the piston immediately. His spark plug is on the side of the cylinder about midway between the pistons (should have said valves), at the top of the stroke and under the cylinder head. This puts his ignition point directly in the cylinder proper. Compare this with the fashionable type of valve chambers, sometimes two or three inches from the cylinder pipe, and it is easily seen that quick burning of the gases is arrived at, with the pressure exerted quickly and immediately upon the pistons, and that all these points tend to give better efficiency. The fashionable type is good for a lot of things, but it is perfectly sure that the quicker you burn the gas the quicker you fill your cylinders, the better the horsepower achieved.

David and Tom were enthusiastic upon their return to Flint from New York on January 23, 1905. "The Buick car was the sensation in its class," said David. The car was to be exhibited that very week at the Philadelphia auto show.

Decades later, when an elderly Durant was attempting to write his autobiography, he unfortunately did not get around to writing the Buick chapter, though his outline did lay out plans for one. But he did manage to record one Buick anecdote – and it was about the engine.

Durant said a respected friend went on record opposing Durant's move into automobiles in general and Buick's two-cylinder valve-in-head "high-speed" motor in particular. So Durant hired an engine expert named Simmons who studied the Buick engine and came back with a report it was "basically unsound and extremely dangerous and was likely to explode." Trying to be funny, Simmons suggested that anyone who bought one of the engines should also buy a bushel basket to pick the pieces.

Durant noted the high-revving engine was "the product of Arthur Mason," Buick's production manager. Durant recalled Mason became annoyed as he listened to Simmons. Finally Mason responded: "This motor is the culmination of long study, experiments and sleepless nights and I have the utmost confidence in it." Mason then started the engine and put his head alongside. "If it explodes," he said, "I might as well go with it." Simmons left in a huff.

Durant concluded: "Needless to say Mason's work was crowned by a great success and was largely responsible for Buick's quick recognition as a leading motorcar, and his theory adopted by automobile manufacturers all over the world."

The story is repeated as Durant's only written Buick remembrance, but its accuracy is questionable. Mason appears to be now getting too much credit for the Buick engine. Whatever happened to the earlier work of David Buick, Walter Marr and Eugene Richard? The story also has a made-up quality that sounds like a shortened version of Dolnar's claims and critics. Further, Durant named the respected friend who first warned him as Col. William McCreery, a prominent local figure who was a hero for escaping the Confederate Libby Prison during the Civil War. Durant was a young admirer of McCreery, and no doubt wanted him in his autobiography. But in fact McCreery had died on December 9, 1896 – nearly a decade before he could possibly have talked to Durant about Buick engines.

By 1905, David Buick and his family were getting settled in Flint. The family had moved to that city in September of 1904, leasing a house from businessman Flint P. Smith at E. Kearsley and Stevens streets, and selling his place on Meldrum in Detroit by year's end.

In June of 1905, Flint's civic leaders created a big celebration in honor of its 50th anniversary as a city. Tom Buick was on the Committee on New Flint along with James H. Whiting, William S. Ballenger and Charles W. Nash. (The event's Reception Committee included Billy Durant, his attorney, John J. Carton, carriage maker William A. Paterson and Flint banker Arthur G. Bishop).

A highlight of the Golden Jubilee was a parade down Saginaw Street with U.S. Vice President Charles W. Fairbanks waving to the large crowd from a carriage. Carl Crow, in *The City of Flint Grows Up,* pointed out "one of the features of the parade was a new car driven by a daughter of Dave Buick, one of the first women in the United States to drive a car."

Crow added a personal observation: "A local reporter was so excited by this unusual spectacle that he described the car as being filled with yellow chrysanthemums. This does not appear probable for the parade was held in June – some months before chrysanthemums were in bloom. The reporter's error was unimportant..." The reporter's error was nonexistent. A photo of the parade unmistakenly shows two 1905 Model C Buicks covered with the flowers.

Indeed, Buick's elder daughter, Frances Jane, won an award for her decoration of the car. Surprisingly, however, it was her younger sister, Mabel Lucille, who drove the Buick in the parade. Frances Jane was a passenger along with Miss Jennie Dullam and a Miss Fenton. The second flower-bedecked Buick, just behind Mabel's car in the photo, was driven by Flint P. Smith, who had bought it in April.

But David's time in the sun in the Buick organization was growing short. Before the end of 1905, it became apparent Durant was beginning to lean more on Marr than on David for mechanical expertise. Late in the year, Durant and Carton needed to list the assets that would justify a boost in Buick's capitalization from $500,000 to $1.5 million. Finding himself $60,000 short when he added them up, Carton assigned that amount of value to contracts between Durant and Marr for "the exclusive use by said W. C. Durant of improvements in explosive engine construction, invented by said Walter L. Marr,

Covered with chrysanthemums, a 1905 Model C Buick is driven by David Buick's daughter, Mabel Lucille, during the 1905 Golden Jubilee parade celebrating Flint's 50 years as a city. Buick's other daughter, Frances Jane, is one of the other young women in the car. Behind them, another 1905 Buick, this one covered with roses, is driven by its owner, Flint P. Smith. The parade featured U.S. Vice President Charles W. Fairbanks.

but on account of business reasons not patented..." Carton's use of Marr's name, rather than David Buick's, made it clear Marr was now recognized within the company as its mechanical innovator.

(The language for such intangible assets, by the way, was questionable. But Carton's excellent connections in Michigan government allowed the explanation to stand. Carton had been Speaker of the of the House in the state Legislature in 1901 and 1903 and would be president of the state Constitutional Convention of 1907-08.)

There was also no question about who was in charge at Buick Motor Company. William Beacraft remembered the situation when he arrived in Flint in late 1903 as Arthur Mason's engine foreman and master mechanic, at a time the company had only 40 employees: "We were just struggling along then, and it was not until the second week of my arrival that I hired an assistant. In the spring of 1904 we put out our first cars....Our first thought then was whether we could sell the cars when we made them, but this soon reversed itself to: how can we get them out fast enough to supply the demand?

139

David Buick's Marvelous Motor Car

"It was when W. C. Durant took hold that the company was reorganized and took on new life…. In those days we were so busy that I used to sleep in the shop, but we never could keep up with the demand…"

Chapter 12

Buick thrives, but where's the founder?

With Billy Durant in control of Buick Motor Company, the next few years were charged with energy. As Ben Briscoe wrote in 1921, the period after Durant's 1904 takeover was "so fraught with romance that it made the Arabian Nights look commonplace."

As for David Buick, it's ironic he was overshadowed by Durant and virtually becomes lost in the historical record, because his name would hardly be remembered at all if Durant hadn't built the company into a giant.

Though engine production remained in Flint, Durant moved Buick's assembly operations in early 1905 to a large and vacant plant owned by the Durant-Dort Carriage Company in Jackson, Mich. About 750 Model C Buicks were built in Jackson that year.

Durant used some of the $325,000 in stock he had been given by the shareholders to finance the move to Jackson. He transferred $101,000 to Whiting and $22,000 to Begole in exchange for their personal management of the Buick company. Whiting took charge of Buick in Jackson and Begole helped manage the Jackson and Flint operations.

(Whiting was later criticized by Ballenger and several other stockholders who filed a legal complaint in 1911 contending Whiting had cut a secret deal with Durant at the time Whiting was helping Durant raise capitalization to $500,000. Both Whiting and Durant denied it. Durant said it was only after he gained control of Buick that he realized he needed management help and in December of 1904 arranged with Whiting to go to Jackson to manage operations there and with Begole to help manage the firm in Flint as well as Jackson).

Durant turned over some of his Buick stock to the Durant-Dort Carriage Company, partly in payment for use of the Jackson plant, and partly because, as he pointed out, he was promoting Buick on the carriage company's time. According to the respected auto writer W. A. P. John, Durant used the rest to get Buick out of debt. "When the banks were extricated and all obligations settled, only $75,000 of the $500,000 remained. And it was from this specific picayune sum that the whole of General Motors, with its countless millions, sprang," John wrote in *Motor* magazine in January 1923.

Early in 1905, after the move of Buick assembly to Jackson, Durant raised another $500,000, mostly from his business associates in Flint, to build a gargantuan complex of factories on Flint's north side. Most of the financial supporters, Durant pointed out, had never ridden in an automobile.

They came up with the money to assure Durant would move the whole Buick business back to Flint – and not leave it at Jackson or move it to Bay City or one of the other sites he had investigated. Some of the investors were Durant's wealthy uncles and cousins. Money generated decades earlier by Henry Crapo's lumber operations would now help finance the big new opportunity of the early 20th century. Others included Flint banks and even Durant's partner, Dallas Dort. Among the big investors was the Durant-Dort Carriage Company itself, which pledged $100,000.

Workers poured into Flint by the thousands, first building the complex and then building Buicks. The new Buick complex, called the Oak Park Plant, was situated on the 220-acre farm of lumberman William Hamilton, a combination of open farm land and scrub oak, with railroad access, which Durant had bought for $22,000 for expansion of the Durant-Dort Carriage Company around 1900 and which was sold to Buick Motor Company in 1905.

When the first phase of the complex was completed by 1907, it encompassed an office building, three factories and a garage, some still under construction and all owned by the Buick firm, situated in the center of a group of 10 factories. The others were owned and operated by companies manufacturing bodies, springs, wheels and castings – "a part of the product of each outside factory being purchased by the Buick Motor Company," an auditor reported. The "Buick City" idea of a main plant to build the entire car, with supplier factories

Billy Durant (light cap in front seat) in a 1906 Buick Model F. This was during the 1906 Glidden Tour, two years before Durant used Buick as the foundation when he created General Motors.

closely aligned, arrived with fanfare in Flint in 1984, but Durant had first demonstrated the concept on the same site about eight decades earlier – and very successfully.

The auditor, J. W. Wellington, checking the property for Ben Briscoe at a time Briscoe wanted to join Durant in a consolidation of companies, said in 1908 that all the buildings "complete what is probably the finest equipment in the Country for the manufacture and sale of automobiles." Wellington's conclusion: "The business as a whole is in excellent condition and can be developed to give magnificent results with an extremely large factory output, a great volume of sales and excellent profits."

The factories quickly ran two and three shifts as production soared. Starting with 37 Model Bs built on W. Kearsley in Flint in 1904 and 750 Model Cs assembled in Jackson in 1905, Buick production rose to 1,400 in Jackson in 1906, to 4,641 after the new Flint complex opened in 1907 and to 8,820 in 1908. By 1910, production reached 30,525. The Model B of 1904, Model C of 1905 and Model F of 1906 were essentially the same and no doubt featured more of David Buick's input than any other production Buick.

The valve-in-head Model B engine was the product of David's

143

team, which was said to include, besides the earlier work of Richard and/or Marr, major engineering and design by Mason and Beacraft. Marr, having persuaded Whiting to consider building cars according to his own recollection, took charge of planning the total vehicle. David was said to have designed the body, which was built of wood by the Flint Wagon Works. Perhaps it was David who found those quirky steel front fenders that show up only on the models B and C.

The Model B was classified as a light touring automobile, weighing 1,675 pounds. The five-passenger side-entrance body was finished in dark blue. The engine was a two-cylinder valve-in-head of 4.5 by 5 bore and stroke developing up to 21 horsepower at 1230 rpm. The price was $950.*

By the time Buick automobile production was transferred to Jackson and the 1905 Model C moved into production, Buick was claiming it "has more speed, more power, more room and style and less vibration, and makes less noise and trouble than any other car in its class on the market."

On May 10, 1905, when David again gave a production report to the *Flint Daily News,* it described his duties as "in charge of the Jackson end of the Buick Motor Company" (although Whiting actually had that job). Said Buick: "We shipped 53 machines last week, and the output this week will be 70 machines." By then, the decision to build the new Flint complex had been made. "The Jackson plant will be kept in operation until the enlarged Flint plant is in readiness for operation, probably about the first of next January," he said.

---

* A notable aspect of the 1904 engine was the location of its pushrods. They were positioned on the bottom. Some buyers of the engine complained that the pushrods caused trouble – dirt collecting on the rods would foul the engine. For 1905, the Model C engine was turned around so the pushrods were on the top, which allowed less oil to drip out and less dirt to creep in. Said Mason: "We just flopped the old engine bottom-side up." Only two of the 1904 Model B pushrods-on-bottom engines are known to exist. One is now in a replica of the first Flint Buick, the Model B that was only a chassis without body or fenders when Marr and Tom Buick drove it round-trip to Detroit in July of 1904. The replica at this writing is being rebuilt for display in the Buick Gallery and Research Center of Flint's Sloan Museum. The other 1904 engine is in private ownership, the centerpiece of a Model B created just in time for Buick's 2003 centennial.

Buick thrives, but where's the founder?

By 1907, there were more new models. Besides the Model F, which was the Model C successor, and the G runabout, both of which debuted in 1906, there were now the models D, H, S and K. These four were all four-cylinder 1907 models.

The big product news for 1908 was a nicely styled newcomer – the Model 10. This sporty car was officially described as "a gentleman's light four-cylinder roadster." It was set on an 88-inch wheelbase and powered by a new 3 ¾ by 3 ¾ 165-cubic-inch, overhead-valve engine that generated 22.5 horsepower. The three-passenger car was often referred to as the "White Streak" because it was painted an off-white color called, for some odd reason, Buick gray. It featured bold brass accents, a long and low profile, acetylene headlamps, two-speed planetary transmission, jump-spark ignition and a price of $900. The car quickly grew in popularity because of its appearance, smooth power, ease of control, eventual racing success and price tag.

The Model 10 evolved from Durant's attempt to find a use for the Jackson plant after Buick operations returned to Flint. Durant brought to Jackson a naval armaments engineer named P.R. Janney, whose Janney Motor Company was organized to produce a light four-cylinder engine. The engine proved unsatisfactory, so the business was absorbed by Buick. Walter Marr and his assistant Enos DeWaters redesigned the motor for the Model 10. The Jackson plant was used to build Buick trucks for several years after Buick returned to Flint.

When production of all models totaled 8,820 in 1908, Durant could claim Buick was now the No. 1 producer in the industry – surpassing the combined total of its closest competitors, Ford and Cadillac. Being on top didn't last long because Henry Ford began production of his legendary Model T in the fall of 1908. But for the moment Buick was king. Durant had made the leap from top producer of horse-drawn vehicles to top producer of motor cars.

"Never was there such a man (as Durant)," wrote C.B. Glasscock in *The Gasoline Age* in 1937. "Beside him Henry Ford was a plodding, insignificant, colorless mechanic utterly lacking in romance or drama, without distinction, without charm – the tortoise beside the hare." Glasscock and others credit Durant for linking the auto industry to Wall

145

Model 10 waits for an earlier mode of transportation to pass near Liberty, N.Y.

Street, bringing in much more money as well as stock promotion.

Take a quick look at his accomplishments of the next few years. Thanks to the financial success of Buick, Durant was in position in early 1908 to pull together a group of auto and supplier firms under one umbrella. Durant first met with Ben Briscoe, Buick's original financial angel and at that time head of Maxwell-Briscoe Company, over breakfast at the Dresden Hotel in Flint and then at Buick headquarters there, to discuss a consolidation of car companies in the low-priced field.

For a time the talks also included Henry Ford and Ransom Olds, who by then had left Oldsmobile and was in charge of the REO Motor Car Company. One afternoon in 1908, Durant, Ford and Olds were invited to meet with Briscoe in the old Penobscot Building in Detroit. As Durant recalled: "In the public reception room were gathered the principals, their close associates and advisers. The room was small, no place to discuss business. I sensed, unless we ran to cover, plenty of undesirable publicity in the offing. As I had commodious quarters in the Pontchartrain Hotel, and as the luncheon hour was approaching, I suggested that we separate and meet in my room as soon as convenient. I had the unexpected pleasure of entertaining the entire party until mid-afternoon."

The discussions eventually foundered when Ford and then Ransom Olds demanded cash instead of stock in a new company.

When those talks collapsed, Durant set out on his own. He created a company which he called General Motors, incorporating it September 16, 1908, using unknowns as officers to avoid attention. First he had General Motors buy Buick for $3.75 million, mostly in an exchange of stock, and then Oldsmobile for a little more than $3 million, again mostly in an exchange of stock. After Buick and Olds, Durant then brought in Cadillac, Oakland (Pontiac predecessor), a group of truck firms that would eventually form GMC, and altogether more than 30 automotive and supplier firms.

Durant even backed a young spark plug maker named Albert Champion, whose initials would eventually form a brand name – AC Spark Plug (his name was already on the Champion spark plug from his previous firm). Champion's first base of operations for Durant was in a corner of the new Buick headquarters building on Hamilton Avenue in Flint.

The car that launched GM was Buick and more specifically two models. The first was the original Flint Buick that was introduced as the Model B and evolved into the barely changed Model C (1905) and Model F (1906). The second was the Model 10 of 1908. The models B/C/F were basically the cars created under David Buick's direction by Buick and Marr (with engine design credits to Richard, Marr, Mason and Beacraft). Of 6,828 Buicks produced from 1904 through 1907, most of them – 5,459 – were the models B/C/F. And in 1908 – the year GM was created – there were 3,281 Model Fs out of 8,820 total Buicks.

In 1908, the Model F relinquished Buick production leadership to the new Model 10, of which 4,002 were built that year. Just as the Model F gave Durant the early confidence, momentum and money to create General Motors, the Model 10 – sometimes called the first General Motors car – provided a big boost during the year of GM's creation. (Model 10 production doubled to 8,100 in 1909 and jumped to 11,000 in 1910 before the post-Durant leadership unaccountably killed it off as Buick production fell from 30,525 in 1910 to 13,389 in 1911).

During his early period of assembling companies to form GM, Durant almost bought Ford Motor Company, too. But in 1909 he couldn't persuade banks to loan the $8 million price tag for a firm that was already producing the Model T and would be worth $35 million a few years later. Durant expressed no regrets. He said later he never could have succeeded with Ford to the extent Henry Ford did.

In 1910, Durant was forced from control of General Motors by bankers concerned he was expanding too fast. So he turned to Louis Chevrolet, the former Buick racing star, and formed Chevrolet Motor Company. Then Durant traded stock so he could regain control of GM in 1915-16 – a sensational maneuver that stunned the business world.

Durant surrounded himself with plenty of high-powered men in this period. Among them were Louis and Arthur Chevrolet and Wild Bob Burman of the great Buick racing team, super salesman Charles Howard, one of Teddy Roosevelt's Rough Riders who became Buick's western distributor (and was later famous as the owner of the race horse Seabiscuit), and such leaders as Charles W. Nash and Walter P. Chrysler, both of whom headed Buick before creating marques of their own.

Fred Smith, Oldsmobile's leader at the time Durant bought Olds for General Motors, observed in 1928: "I had at least the intelligence to see in him (Durant) the strongest and most courageous individual then in the business and the master salesman of all time…It would be a poorly posted analyst who failed to list W. C. Durant as the most picturesque, spectacular and aggressive figure in the chronicles of American automobiledom."

So where, in all this, is David Buick?

Durant's daughter, Margery, recalled in a privately published memoir her father's relationship with David. She described Buick as "an inventor he (Durant) had met and liked, and whose invention had interested him." While some of his friends urged him to change the name of the car from Buick to Durant, he declined. She recalled her father musing: "Buick…Buick. Wonder if they'd call it 'Boo-ick?'" But finally he decided he thought the name had appeal, and it honored "the man who invented the engine."

Buick thrives, but where's the founder?

Margery also remembered her father, under a gaslight, drawing a rectangle and then writing the name Buick diagonally, slanting upward to the right.

"Margery, I think that's the name we want," Durant said to his daughter. "And I think that's the way we want to use it." She was defining the creation of the early Buick script logo.

This would have been entirely in character. Durant not only liked to name his products, he particularly relished working on the graphics. For example, the famous "bow-tie" Chevrolet emblem he chose was virtually a copy of a symbol he saw in an illustrated Sunday newspaper in 1913 in Warm Springs, Va., his second wife, Catherine, told the writer. That refutes an old yarn he saw it on wallpaper in Paris. "I was with him," said Catherine. "We were in a suite, reading the papers, and he saw this design and said, 'I think this would be a very good emblem for the Chevrolet.' I'm not sure he said Chevrolet, because I don't think he had even settled on a name yet." Ken Kaufman, an authority on early Chevrolet history, checked out this story by going through Sunday newspapers that would have circulated in Warm Springs at the time. He found a symbol almost the same as the bow-tie in an advertisement for a coal company.

When Durant bought a fledgling refrigerator company in 1918 and later turned it over to GM, he himself thought up the firm's brand name – Frigidaire. Durant also claimed to have created the name General Motors, one of several suggestions he was said to have placed on a list for his lawyers to check out.

Margery noted that when her father defended keeping the Buick name, "perhaps…there jumped into his (Durant's) mind the picture of the little shed where he and I went and listened to Mr. Buick explain the mechanism; just a little outhouse with shelves full of tools and metal parts, greasy and cramped and dark. Just the kind of place you'd think might be the cradle of a great invention. And he'd feel the justice of perpetuating the name…"*

---

* The words reflect the talent of Fitzhugh Green, Margery's ghost writer, who became her husband. One wonders if this "little outhouse" was actually the "barn" in which the first Buick automobile was said to have been built. Another

David Buick's Marvelous Motor Car

Despite such sentiments and amidst all the excitement of rapid sales increases, major racing victories and the beginnings of General Motors, David Buick did get lost. He almost disappears from the record. This tough little Scotsman, who had so carefully controlled and nurtured his tiny businesses, must have been way out of his league in this new environment. There were too many big personalities. There was too much going on. (According to one report, David's reduced stature is indicated by the fact he owned 1,000 shares of Buick stock on March 10, 1904, but only 110 shares on September 9, 1905 – though he may have sold some to help son Tom finance his share of a new brass foundry).

Occasionally his name would surface. There was, for example, the passing mention in 1905 that David was in charge of Buick's Jackson operations. In February 1907, *The Flint Journal* in describing the Buick firm said "the experimental department is one of the most important in the entire factory, and the one over which D.D. Buick himself has personal supervision. The men of this department are among the highest paid of any in the company."

Also, on November 6, 1907, *The Flint Journal* reported the Buick stockholders' annual meeting was held the previous day in the Buick offices. The story said it had been a remarkable year for Buick, and there were predictions of an even better one ahead. It said 50 stockholders were introduced from Chicago, New York, Boston, Detroit, Owosso, Flint and elsewhere. David Buick was listed as among those elected to the board.

But in general, David was shrinking further from the limelight, apparently contenting himself with experimental work. What evidence exists suggests he busied himself with inconsequential projects, building a reputation as a dreamer unable or unwilling to assert himself as the company's founder and namesake.

It's clear the Buick family's status within the company was sliding downward. Tom Buick left the company in 1906 after a dispute with Durant and became more involved with a brass foundry, Auto Brass

---

possibility: the small test shed adjacent to the original Flint Buick plant on W. Kearsley Street.

Buick thrives, but where's the founder?

& Aluminum Company, of which he was part owner. It provided the Buick company with brass parts. When the foundry was organized in 1904, Tom was its secretary. It went bankrupt when the Buick company couldn't pay its bills in a later financial crisis, sending Tom Buick's finances spiraling out of control. In early 1909, Tom was listed as president of Genesee Tire Company in Flint, but later that year he was bankrupt.

Another of Buick's children was at the center of an unpleasant situation. In July of 1905, Buick Motor Company was sued for $5,000 by a woman for a car accident in Jackson involving a daughter of Buick and her friends. Rachel Beadle claimed she was knocked down by one of the company's automobiles which was being shown to a prospective purchaser. The machine was being operated by an "inexperienced woman," apparently the Buick daughter. An officer of the company was with her at the time.

Catherine Durant, second wife of General Motors founder William C. Durant, was Durant's secretary in 1905 when he was taking control of Buick's fortunes. They were married in 1908.

It's unknown whether the suit, filed a month after the Golden Jubilee parade, involved the younger daughter, Mabel, who drove in the parade, or her older sister Frances. The suit was dismissed as without merit, but John Carton, who was Durant's attorney (and sometimes acted as the Buick company's attorney), had trouble collecting $92.58 from David Buick after David said he would handle the bill personally.

Carton insisted on this payment from the man who had given his name to the Buick automobile. Finally Durant stepped in, sending the check, and this note: "Mr. Buick wishes me to say that until a few moments ago this was more money than he had in the world. He disliked very much to make this admission...."

This was apparently in jest – or was it? Durant's letter to Carton continued: "All joking aside, and in fairness to Mr. Buick, I wish to say that the fault is not entirely his. Some time ago we had an understanding with him as to his compensation for the present year and I have only just learned that Mr. Whiting failed to put this into effect on the 1st of October. Mr. Buick wishes me to express his regret that he has been unable to meet this matter earlier and to offer his apology for his neglect for which he feels he has been justly scolded."

So we're left with this picture of Whiting failing to pay David Buick, of Carton harassing him for a minor bill, of Durant stepping in and calling it all a joke. The only thing clear is something was not right with David Buick's relationship with Buick Motor Company at that time.

Fred Hoelzle, interviewed at age 92 by the writer in 1976, worked at Buick when the founder was there. David Buick, said Hoelzle, "never seemed to fit himself in with others. Nobody seemed to take to him. I think he was most interested in finances. He was quiet and we didn't see him very often. Finally, he just kind of faded away. Nobody seemed to notice." That judgment may not be worth much as Hoelzle was probably not often in position to cross paths with Buick. And he incorrectly remembered Buick as a tall man. It's ironic, though, that by 1908, when Buick Motor Company claimed to lead the industry in production, Buick the man had disappeared into the bureaucracy.

His name did surface occasionally. In January of 1906, a fire wiped out the barn of Flint businessman Flint P. Smith. The newspapers reported two cars parked there, each worth $1,200, were destroyed. One was Smith's car, believed to be a 1905 Model C Buick, likely the car bedecked in flowers he had driven in the Golden Jubilee parade. The other car destroyed might have also been a Model C parade vehicle – it had been temporarily parked in Smith's barn by David Buick.

Chapter 13

David Buick hits the road

At some point, it all became too much. David Buick figured it was time to do something else – although that would turn out to be a bad idea. His departure from Buick Motor Company has been variously reported as between 1905 and 1908, though more likely it was between fall 1909 and spring 1910.

After he was re-elected to the Buick board in November 1907, the evidence is slim. A 1930s Buick magazine article describes an early scene in which racing reports were telegraphed to a machine shop at the Buick factory. David was said to be in the shop, nervous, pacing the floor constantly and chewing his cigar as news clattered over the wire. Like most early auto men, David was said to be a big racing fan.

Terry Dunham found enough information to identify the above-mentioned race as the 232-mile Cobe Trophy won by Buick racer Louis Chevrolet on June 18, 1909. So David could have still been with the company then.

If so, it's easy to see how he could have gotten lost in the highly energized Buick organization. This was an incredibly busy period. The automobile was being perfected and there was a virgin market. With Billy Durant leading a sales surge, the factories were pushed to their limits and beyond. This was the period David recalled when he complained to Bruce Catton: "There wasn't an executive in the place who ever knew what time it was…I tell you, the automobile business was a tough one in those days."

If that wasn't enough, Durant, using Buick as the foundation, energetically scooped up more companies as he created the nucleus of a General Motors that would become unbeatable in size in the 20th century and into the early years of the new millennium. He bought so many companies because, he said, he was afraid of missing out on some hot new technology. As Durant explained to A.B.C. Hardy: "How could I tell what these engineers would say next? ...I was for getting every car in sight, playing safe all along the line."

The Buick organization was running at top speed at all levels. Its racing team led by Wild Bob Burman and Louis Chevrolet was hitting its stride as it won 500 trophies from 1908 to 1910.

As the *Detroit News* reported in 1909: "One must see for himself; one must get into the atmosphere of the tremendous undertakings; one must himself walk over the literal miles of factories in process of construction before one begins to grasp the immensity of the manufacturing undertaking that has made Flint, next to Detroit, the automobile center of the world."

A sense of Durant's reputation at this time is revealed by author Arthur Pound. He said lawyer John Carton "wanted me to realize that Billy Durant put no value on money for its own sake; that the founder of General Motors was an unconventional soul who soared high above ordinary humanity, that the one and only Billy...was almost a prince among mortals, enjoying first of all power, then excitement, then the affectionate adulation of his friends."

Evidence of the time of David Buick's departure from all this is an advertisement in the *New York Herald* dated November 6, 1910, in which Buick is quoted: "One year ago my health broke down and I was a physical wreck – so the doctor said. I went to California but I seemed to get no better. I lived in Los Angeles and while I was trying to recover my health I made a study of the oil business...."

That seems a clear statement Buick became ill in late 1909 and then went to California. But another David Buick ad, undated, says he "went to California in April, 1910, in search of health." Somehow, David got the idea he should get into the oil business. In a lawsuit filed in 1914, it was said he made that decision in answer to an advertisement from a man seeking a wealthy partner to invest in California oil properties.

David incorporated Buick Oil Company in California in March of 1910. Either Buick was setting up the business from long distance

David Buick hits the road

David Buick after he left Buick Motor Company, a rare profile from the album of his grandson, David Dunbar Buick II.

or the April date for his arrival in California is wrong. Fall of 1909 seems a more likely date for his departure from Buick Motor Company, though he may have left earlier before traveling to California. David is telling his story in advertisements because the ads are soliciting investors in his oil properties.

In his interview with Bruce Catton, Buick reiterated he left the Buick company because his health had broken. Although he did not specifically blame Durant, several men who worked for Durant were driven to the brink of health breakdowns – or over the brink. One was Durant-Dort President A.B.C. Hardy in the carriage era. He resigned at the point of collapse and took an extended trip to France. Another

David Buick's Marvelous Motor Car

Buick Oil Company stock certificate.

was Walter Marr, who said he was working 22 out of 24 hours a day, ruining his health. And still another was early Frigidaire executive Alfred Mellowes, who said he may not have quit had Durant allowed him a vacation in the north woods.

But this could be unfair to Durant. Industrial history in this period is littered with those who worked to the point of exhaustion just because of the frenetic, exciting challenges of the times – not because they were driven to illness by some unforgiving boss. And the lure of profits in California oil properties may have been a bigger reason than any health problems for David's decision to leave the company and head west.

When David left, Durant reportedly gave him $100,000 – about $2 million in early new millennium dollars – for his stock, though a contradictory report indicates David still had considerable GM stock after his departure. Buick's grandson, David II, said his father, Tom Buick, claimed stock that should have been given to David, and never was, would have been worth $115 million at the time of David's

Buick complex in Flint around 1910, not long after David Buick left the company.

death. Briscoe seems to confirm this, but David II said it may only be a family story. "My father was very bitter about this, but Grandpa (David Buick) never seemed to be."

David gave his version to Catton: "I had a good block of stock. The directors held a meeting the day I left. I was told that they'd voted to pay me my salary the rest of my life. I thought I was all set. But they only paid it for three years. After that, I never got a cent."

According to the grandson, David "didn't hold much animosity toward the Buick company for the way he ended up. I remember that he did own a Buick once…"

The most revealing judgments about David's career at Buick Motor Company come from A.B.C. Hardy and from Durant himself.

Hardy's take was that David was a dreamer who kept experimenting with some new gadget without applying his talents to the business of manufacturing a marketable motor car.

And Durant gave his view to George H. Maines, a prominent public relations executive whose father developed property near the Buick factory into homes for the workers and their families.

"David Buick was a likeable fellow," Durant told Maines. "But he was a dreamer, and he couldn't be practical…We did everything we could at the plant to make it easy for him. We arranged for his son, Tom, to be on the payroll, and to try to keep his father settled, but after some years he just drifted away."

David Buick's Marvelous Motor Car

It's understandable why he may have wanted to leave. The situation must have been suffocating to his ego. While others made millions on the company that carried his name, David had struggled financially. But with the reported settlement with Durant, David might well have now gone home to Detroit – or even to California – and taken up boating again, enjoying a comfortable early retirement at the age of 55. But David Buick seldom took the easy path.

Chapter 14

Oil in California

In his first 55 years, David Buick seldom displayed much appetite for personal promotion. Indeed he was so quiet he largely disappeared from everyone's radar screens, including those of the leaders of Buick Motor Company.

But by the time he arrived in Los Angeles after half a century of living in Detroit and Flint, Mich., he was virtually being marketed as David Buick – Superstar! Advertisements soliciting investors in his new-found oil properties suggested this was a successful and very wealthy businessman who had stepped away from thousands of admiring workers in Flint only because his health had failed and he needed a warmer climate.

The ads, appearing in late 1910 in newspapers in New York, Chicago, Toronto and probably elsewhere, were big and sensational. One, displaying a portrait of David Buick, was headlined, "Buick Makes Fortune in Oil." It sought "conservative investors" willing to back David's dollars with theirs. "He is not a poor man with a promising future," the ads assured. "Buick is a rich man, with a lifelong list of business successes to his credit…. As a businessman who does not let his enthusiasm run away with his common sense, he…knows he will get it all back many times over."

One of the ads was a virtual "advertorial," several pages in *The Strand Magazine,* in what looked like a magazine article, complete with a byline, except with a coupon for more information at the end. After praising the character and the successes of David Buick, the "article" described Buick's old plumbing supply business, Buick & Sherwood, as at one time "the largest plumbing supply house in the world." David was "now heavily interested in the General Motors Co., the largest corporation of its kind in the world." Furthermore,

159

David Buick's Marvelous Motor Car

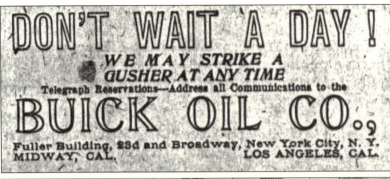

Buick Oil Company solicitation ads starting 1910.

"to the automobile trade he has always been known as a practicer of the Square Deal...."

In Flint, though Buick Motor Company was driving the economy, the big names linked to the company were Durant, Whiting, Mason, Begole and maybe the new general manager, Big Bill Little. Buick the man was hardly a public personality. But the magazine ad proclaimed: "15,000 workingmen in Flint, Michigan, know this man and his business ideals."

David Buick's automobile had finally made him famous about

Oil in California

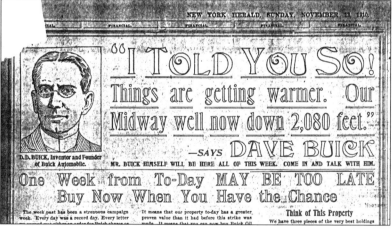

the time he left it. Now he was either being surrounded by people who saw his name as a ticket to success, or he himself was deeply involved in building his image and creating aggressive oil promotions. Probably some of both.

Most information about David's California years comes from those who were either promoting or attacking him. In one lawsuit, it was alleged Buick Oil Company "from the beginning was impregnated with fraud…." On the other hand, Buick Oil Company officials loyal to David stated he and his associates strongly opposed "reprehensible" advertising.

The basic facts were David Buick incorporated Buick Oil Company March 4, 1910, with four Californians – J.B. Lehigh, Stacy C. Lamb and Walter Rose, all of Los Angeles, and John M. Herndon of South Pasadena – and that firm quickly acquired an option on 640 acres of oil-rich property, the "Buick Midway Holdings," in Kern County, north of L.A.

According to a 1914 lawsuit, Herndon and Lehigh were promoters of oil and mineral lands. Herndon advertised for a wealthy partner to invest in oil lands and David responded. Together they put up $20,000 for an option to buy the Kern County acreage.

By 1913 David was boasting of big successes, and no wonder. If you wanted to be in oil, Kern County was a good place to be. Oil had been oozing to the surface there from ancient times. In the 1700s, Indians used tar from local pits for trading, waterproofing and as an adhesive. In the mid 1800s, entrepreneurs were digging shallow pits and refining tar into lamp kerosene. Next came tunnels and mines, then wells. A new chapter began in 1896 when the Shamrock gusher blew, sending 1,300 barrels of oil flowing per day, according to the San Joaquin Geological Society. This was good timing as the gasoline engine was a very important – and very thirsty – new arrival on the world industrial scene.

If solicitation ads were accurate, one Buick Oil Company well produced 900,000 barrels of oil in 10 months. Another came in as a gusher and produced 500,000 barrels in four months. David called it "one of the most sensational gushers in the history of California oil."

News stories supported some of the claims. An article in the *Los Angeles Times* on January 14, 1912, that was headlined "Buick Gusher is Beyond Control," reported the well was "shooting a stream of oil high over the derrick," an awesome sight captured in a photograph. But a few months later, another article reported Buick Oil Company was trying to deny this well was "ruined by water infiltration of the rich gusher sands."

Such reports were not true, according to the Buick firm. Standard Oil Company, which had a contract with Buick Oil Company, said the percentage of water and other contaminants in the Buick oil was

Oil in California

Terry B. Dunham

Buick Oil Company hits a gusher in California in 1912.

acceptable – from 1 percent to not more than 3 percent. At the same time this was reported, Buick Oil Company announced a 4 per cent dividend, which reportedly placed it "in the front ranks as a dividend payer." (There must have been something to the rumors about the wells, though. In 1915, the company acknowledged its first well "sanded up" in January of 1912 and two others in April 1912 and February 1913.)

At one point, David described himself as president and chief stockholder of a successful gold mining company "operating on the

163

mother lode" in Tuolumne County, California. That firm was not recorded by the California secretary of state, but overall, Buick painted a picture of success. David Buick wanted very much to be seen as wealthy. "Since locating in Los Angeles, Mr. Buick has built a handsome home in one of the fashionable residence sections of the city and his family has taken an active part in the social life in California," his 1913 biographical sketch revealed. It also noted:

> While he is distinguished for having made a success in all his ventures, Mr. Buick's greatest success came to him late in life, for he was forty-nine years of age when he organized the Buick Motor Company; but since that time all of his ventures have been attended with extraordinarily large rewards.

When David first went to Los Angeles in 1910, he lived at 3016 S. Western Avenue. By 1911, he and his family lived in a house at 446 S. St. Andrews Place, near Wilshire Boulevard and Western. Apparently he liked the neighborhood, because a year or two later, David built a house at 350 S. St. Andrews.

Buick's younger daughter, Mabel Lucille, lived with her parents until she married James Duryea Coyle, a native of San Francisco and president of James D. Coyle Realty Company of Los Angeles, on April 9, 1912. Miss Buick "formerly resided in Detroit and Flint, Mich., where she was well known in society circles," said a notice of an engagement party given by Mr. and Mrs. Buick at their Los Angeles home (at that time 446 S. St. Andrews). The couple planned to live in Los Angeles after a honeymoon in Honolulu.*

As for the oil business, David's ads soliciting investors described his observations and experiences at some length. David had learned, one ad said, the oil business didn't take much labor – three men were working nine wells and could handle many times that

---

* The elder daughter, Frances Jane, after an early divorce married Frank Patterson, a one-time shoe salesman from New York who was eventually involved in the oil business. They had one daughter, Caroline Louisa Patterson, who married Warren Boes. Their son, Doug Boes, remembers his grandmother, Frances Jane, lived with them for a time. The only family treasures that came down to him were a set of silverware from a Flint firm, decorated with the letter "B" stamped on each item, and the small brass cannon David had used as a starting gun for regattas in his early Detroit days.

number. He became as fascinated with oil as he had earlier with engines and automobiles. "The question of oil was so interesting and so absorbing to me that I could not think of anything else," he was quoted as saying. It was explained he was spending all of his time in the oil fields, using his engineering experience to direct operations first hand.

In some ads, potential investors were warned to act quickly if they really wanted to make money: "One week from today may be too late."

And then came the headline in the *New York Times* on November 22, 1910.

"Postal Raids Show Vast Stock Frauds."

U.S. Post Office inspectors and police detectives had raided two of the largest sales agencies of unlisted stock in New York City and arrested four men "prominently identified with the distribution of stock in oil companies, wireless concerns, mining and other enterprises...." The raids were part of a crusade "with the approval of President Taft" to wipe out swindling operations through the mails "which in the last five years…have filched from the public more than $100,000,000," the newspaper reported. One raided outfit was Burr Brothers, a firm whose president, Sheldon C. Burr, was arrested along with two other company officials.

Buick Oil Company was only one of a large number of companies listed in the article, with postal authorities noting Burr Brothers had recently been advertising its stock. David Buick, however, managed to stumble prominently into the story:

> Yesterday afternoon while Inspector (T.M.) Reddy was in the office of the Burr Brothers, there came a long-distance call on the telephone for S.C. Burr. The man at the other end announced that he was David Buick, head of the Buick Oil Company and that he was at Flint, Mich.
>
> "What's all this I hear about Burr Brothers getting into trouble?" he asked. Inspector Reddy told him. Mr. Buick asked that a telegram be sent to him at once telling him what had happened and stating whether the Buick Oil Company had been drawn into the matter in any way.

"I'm not here to send you any telegrams," said Inspector Reddy. "If you want information you had better come here and get it."

David Buick's involvement was hardly ignored by the automotive press. A week later (November 30, 1910), *The Horseless Age* weighed in with a story headlined: "Buick's Oil Venture Gets Black Eye"

> When the postal authorities swooped down upon the get-rich-quick scheme of Burr Brothers, of New York city, David R. (sic) Buick, of Flint, Mich., whose name one of the General Motors Company's cars bears, and head of the Buick Oil Company, was considerably annoyed, especially when he heard of the arrest of the members of the Burr Brothers' outfit. This company, which has promoted a number of great schemes for separating the public from its money...were selling agents for the Buick Oil Company. Upon learning the state of affairs, Buick started for New York, and the morning after the raid, had a long talk with Assistant United States Attorney Dorr. To the latter Buick declared that he was quite ignorant of the business records of the men he selected to sell his stock, and that picking Burr Brothers was an error of judgment.
>
> The episode has no bearing on the automobile business, save that the prosperous condition of the industry and the name "Buick" were used as capital by the oil agents to interest "come-ons." The latter were somewhat falsely led to believe that David Buick was the big man of the Buick Motor Car Company, and that he was a great factor in the automobile world. Also that great quantities of refined Buick oil would soon be consumed for lubricating and fuel purposes, not only by owners of Buick cars, but by motorists generally, which naturally would yield enormous dividends. Thousands of "easy" ones bit at the bait.
>
> Just why Buick permitted his name to be connected with such a wildcat scheme without first investigating thoroughly has caused much talk in automobile circles. Just what effect the arrest of the agents will have on the oil concern itself has not yet been determined.

That was far from the end of it. David's oil ventures were becoming more widely noted for legal entanglements than for oil gushers. A geologist, Ralph Arnold, filed suit in Superior Court in Los Angeles on January 26, 1912, alleging he had been promised a one-quarter share of the company for his work in finding oil reserves but had received nothing. He was seeking $375,000 plus other damages.

Arnold was not your average geologist. He was the son of a famous Pasadena scientist (the late Delos Arnold) and, according to a news story, "had played with mastadon bones in his nursery." When he went to Stanford, Arnold was said to have known more about fossils than the professors – and almost as much about geology.

Later, as a member of the U.S. Geological Survey, he made maps for the government and wrote bulletins describing all of the oil lands in California. "He has defined the limits and determined the zones of all the oil country in California and has written enough oil and mineral bulletins to fill several five-foot shelves," the article reported.

Arnold was touted in Washington as the leading oil expert on the Pacific Coast and "is busy every minute at $100 a day, according to his attorneys, and is on the staff of the Mexican Petroleum Company, the Union Oil Company and a dozen other large corporations, including an English syndicate which has taken him to Europe twice within the last year."

And now Ralph Arnold was a victim of Buick Oil Company, a story recounted in Los Angeles under the headline: "His Reward a Freeze-out?" One of the subheads: "Automobile King Is Among the Defendants."

This did not look good for Buick, but untangling the Arnold problem created another. A federal lawsuit filed in 1914 by disgruntled Buick Oil Company shareholders complained about the way Buick and John M. Miner, who was described in the suit as "Buick's alleged attorney," settled with Arnold. Buick and Miner agreed, according to the suit, to pay him $10,000 in cash from the company treasury and transfer to him 100,000 shares of Buick Oil Company stock. The stockholders' attorney, Alfred E. Case of Chicago, contended Buick and John Herndon had entered into the agreement with Arnold before the oil company was organized, and therefore the decision to use company assets to settle the Arnold claim was fraudulent. The attorney argued the stock transfer should be voided and the $10,000 returned to the oil company's treasurer.

There is no file on what could have been Buick's obvious answer – that Arnold's work had probably led to the Buick Oil Company's early successes.

Arnold's was one of several lawsuits attacking Buick Oil Company. Also in 1912, a suit was filed by Benjamin F. Moffatt, demanding the return to him of a large block of the company's stock. And on April 15, 1914, the complaint filed by Case on behalf of the disgruntled stockholders demanded – besides action in the Arnold case among other things – a receivership for the company.

Buick Oil Company responded aggressively. In the Moffatt case, Fred Van Orman, company secretary, alleged Moffatt and the Burr Brothers (one of the firms raided in New York) had secured allotments of the company's stock and were selling it "in the most reckless and unwarrantable manner, realizing profits ranging from 100 to 600 percent."

Said Van Orman: "Their methods were so reprehensible that in the Moffatt case, the company took extreme measures to put a stop to his methods by refusing to make further transfers of stock for him until he had promised the company that he would desist from further questionable advertising."

And in the case brought by the disgruntled stockholders, Buick Oil Company lawyers persuaded a federal judge the complaint had little merit. A news report said the judge issued "a stinging rebuke" to those filing the complaint. The judge held that 70 pages were filled with "scandalous, redundant and impertinent matter" that should be stricken from the record. But he did grant attorney Case time to prepare a new bill of complaint.

This amended bill was filed by Case on April 21, 1915, in federal court in Los Angeles. The stockholders he represented, who had formed the Buick Oil Association to pursue the legal action, lived in 20 states and three Canadian provinces, as well as Australia and Scotland, and represented 500,000 shares of the company's stock.

Oil in California

In summary, Case alleged David Buick had devised a scheme to control valuable oil properties in California without having to pay for them himself, had falsely represented himself as far more wealthy than he was, and that, after incorporating Buick Oil Company, had worked with his "cronies" to manipulate the company's stocks and improperly spend the company's money. The attorney, listing company officers David Buick, John Herndon, John Miner and Fred Van Orman among defendants, alleged no reports of many sales were made and that false and fraudulent statements were made in regard to the value of the stock.

Case told the association that after Herndon and Buick optioned the Kern County property, Buick organized his own company with $5 million capitalization. This firm, Buick Oil Company, issued to David Buick and Herndon three million shares of stock in return for the option on the property. Each took one million shares and transferred one million to J.B. Lehigh, another of the company's directors. They planned to sell a sufficient amount of the other two million shares to the public "to bring in the wells and for other purposes."

Case's numerous letters and telegrams to representatives of the association focused on three subjects: (1) David Buick and his associates had engaged in illegal activities; (2) Case's legal actions against them would assuredly lead to victories that would boost the value of Buick Oil Company stock; and (3) Case needed more money from the association if he were to continue the fight. As time went on, it appeared No. 3 rose to the top of Case's concerns.

In reply, Buick Oil Company said its actions were legal, that the stockholders had failed to complain about alleged illegal actions by normal routes, and it was untrue that Buick, Miner and Van Orman had a scheme to wreck the company "and stop the flow of oil."

Meanwhile, the negative news about Buick Oil Company did not play well back in Flint, at Buick Motor Company. William C. Durant had been temporarily pushed aside in 1910 as bankers took over two-year-old General Motors (he would make a triumphant return to power at GM five years later) and one of Durant's old subordinates at the Durant-Dort Carriage Company, Charles W. Nash, was in charge

David Buick's Marvelous Motor Car

Walter Chrysler (left) and Charles Nash (right) with Walter Marr and his Cyclecar, a 1915 Buick concept. David Buick criticized its configuration in a letter to Marr.

at Buick. On December 19, 1912, Nash responded in a letter to a question about Buick and the oil venture from Fred Warner, head of Buick operations in Chicago. Nash stiffly replied that any reference to David Buick or his oil company in connection with Buick Motor Company "is too absurd to hardly deserve thought."

Nash described Buick as a man "without means" who had persuaded the Flint Wagon Works to invest in a two-cylinder automobile motor designed by Walter Marr. "After they got in quite a ways and needed money Mr. Durant came upon the scene and properly financed the proposition, and the outcome of that has been what you see in the Buick Motor Company of today."

Nash continued: "After two or three years Mr. Buick, who had received some Buick Motor Company stock for what he had done in the matter, disposed of his stock and all his relations with the Buick Motor Company to promote this oil deal of which you read so much. Mr. Buick has had no connection whatever with the Buick Motor Company for the last five years. In fact, I think it is safe to say that he never has entered the Buick Motor Company's office or plant during that time. Therefore, you can see what connection he has had with the Buick Motor Company."

Despite mounting troubles, David himself seemed affable in a long letter to Walter Marr in 1913. He described himself as a booster of Los Angeles. "I like both the warm days and the cool nights for the reasons you can go to bed and sleep every minute; something that you can't do in the east when you have a very hot day," he wrote.

At that time Marr was working on his Cyclecar, a concept compact car of the times, the idea being to create an economy model. It was a narrow vehicle with the passenger seated behind the driver. "I have talked to a great many people," Buick wrote. "And without a single exception they all prefer the seats along side of each other and claim that the tandem seats would not take at all. Of course you will understand all of this is for your information as I do not wish to influence you in any way…." Marr ignored the advice. He built his Cyclecar in 1914 with one seat behind the other. It still exists. But the concept never went anywhere.

Neither, for that matter, did the Buick Oil Company. Case, the attorney representing the disgruntled stockholders, engaged in a long court fight with the company, which battled back with "eight or ten of what are supposed to be the best lawyers in the city," Case said. One newspaper article said an upcoming hearing "promises to furnish a fine display of daylight fireworks if the predictions of the attorneys are verified." Another reported: "The affairs of the Buick Oil Company are a fruitful source of trouble in the local Federal Court, and every time the matter is brought up, it requires the efforts of all the peace conservers concerned to keep the attorneys from each other's throats."

Beginning in early 1914 and continuing into the spring of 1915, letters and telegrams flew back and forth between Case and the representatives of the association of disgruntled stockholders. Most were between Case and the association's secretary, George Kyles, who, like Case, lived in Chicago. Some were between Kyles and the stockholders.

Some letters from Case attacked Buick Oil Company and David Buick. Sometimes Case predicted victory in the courts. April 16, 1914, Case to Kyles: "I have them (Buick Oil Company) on the run." April 22, 1914, Case to Kyles: "Criminal matters under consideration." May 27, 1914, Case to Kyles: "I know I can win and clean the pirates out root and branch... The policy of the law is 'to the diligent litigant belongs the spoils.'"

But often, Case was looking for more money from his clients: May 22, 1914, Case telegram to Kyles (punctuation added): "Can't pay hotel bills...court costs...expenses...keep two families six horses two dogs...make millions from defunct corporations for stockholders on blue sky for the glory of it...cash exhausted...hotel bills due Sunday...money was to be here Tuesday... if Association can't raise funds must quit." June 9, 1914, Case to Kyles: "Money almost gone, bills are overdue." June 10, 1914, Case to Kyles, predicting it is "practically assured" the Buick Oil Company officers will be indicted "but I will or must have money."

By September 15, 1914, Kyles was pleading with the stockholders to send more expense money to Case: "Mr. Case must be back in California in three weeks. You are not so cheap that you would ask him to walk out there, and then sleep in the parks after he gets there. He is fighting your battle...."

On January 8, 1915, Case told A. H. Wolyn, a stockholder whose complaint originally triggered the lawsuit: "I have assured you we will win and we will if you don't drive me from the field." And on February 2, Case informed Kyles he had been told "Buick has quit and that Miner is really the only one in the game. I can assure you I am confident his days are numbered."

Oil in California

David Buick had apparently reacted at Buick Oil Company almost as he had at Buick Motor Company. When things began to go wrong, he became quiet, and then he disappeared from view, and then he left.

The whole show was about over anyway. By then, events were coming to a head between Case and the association. On February 16, 1915, Case wrote to Kyles: "I hope the sheckels are coming in as I am about three weeks behind in my hotel bill...If the Court does not do something pretty soon I am liable to start something, as I become very active when aroused. Everything seems to be working for our advantage but it is too slow for my nerves."

Too slow for the association's, too. Perhaps under pressure from stockholders, Kyles asked for an accounting of Case's expenses. Case's response, on February 17, was explosive: "Do you imagine that I am a slave of yours, to be dictated to and through you, of how and what I shall do, how I shall spend my money, what I shall eat, where I shall stop, where I shall sleep? By reason of your letter I feel that I am relieved from looking after the affairs of the Association any further...."

Case hung around long enough to file the amended bill of complaint on April 21, 1915, but again there was no quick action. A. H. Wolyn decided he had seen enough. In a motion to dismiss the suit, Wolyn revealed numerous letters from Case, including the quotes above, noting they were merely examples of many on the subject of Case's continual demands for expense money.

Wolyn noted Case had given the association "profuse promises to win for them some substantial returns for the outlays of money they were sending to him" and had often threatened to abandon his efforts if funds were not forthcoming. In total, about $2,200 was provided to Case by the association, Wolyn said. It seems not overly expensive, even in 1915 dollars, for a Chicago lawyer working a case for more than a year in California, but it was more than the association – which had seen none of the promised results – wanted to spend.

On September 25, 1915, Wolyn told the association Case had been discharged as its attorney and that the association had directed that the lawsuit against Buick Oil Company be dismissed. With both sides agreeing, the case was officially dismissed on December 28, 1915.

But the damage was done. With all of the expensive litigation, the company was wrecked. And there would be more bad news for David Buick, who would soon leave California. As one news magazine reported: "With what he saved from the oil disaster, Mr. Buick went into real estate. He became a partner in a company that controlled many acres. Unfortunately, they were Florida acres, and when the Florida boom collapsed, the last of Mr. Buick's fortune went with it."

Chapter 15

The final years

By the time David Buick reached his late 60s in the early 1920s, he was virtually broke. His last name, however, was marching on to great success. The Buick automobile had become ever stronger under extraordinary, even legendary, successive leaders – William C. Durant, Charles W. Nash, Walter P. Chrysler and Harry H. Bassett – as well as the brilliant chief engineers Walter L. Marr and his eventual successor, Enos A. DeWaters.

This was despite considerable turmoil. When Durant returned to full power at GM in the spring of 1916, Nash resigned – old business associates and friends parting, except for infrequent personal meetings, for the last time. Nash, originally hired by Durant as a laborer in the Flint Road Cart Company, had risen to vice president and general manager of the Durant-Dort Carriage Company before Durant urged that he be made head of Buick when the bankers took over GM in 1910.

Nash's leadership qualities were quickly recognized by the bankers' board; soon he was president of General Motors. Chrysler, the successful assistant works manager of American Locomotive's plant in Pittsburgh, was brought in by Nash as Buick works manager in 1911. This was at the request of James J. Storrow, interim president of GM under the bankers' board. Storrow felt Nash needed a strong manufacturing man to continue development of GM's most important division.

When Durant returned to control of GM, he asked Nash to stay on as GM president, but Nash wanted none of it – he knew Durant would be making all the decisions. Durant, put off by what he saw as Nash's lack of loyalty to his old boss and benefactor, was not upset by his departure. Storrow, a major adversary of Durant, had predicted Nash's departure in a letter to a business associate on September 24, 1915: "If a good opportunity comes along…I shall resign (from the GM board).

If things do not seem to be going smoothly or well, Mr. Nash undoubtedly will resign also. I felt obliged to make the fight (his unsuccessful effort to to keep the bankers in control of GM) because it seemed to me we could not permit the Company to be turned over to Mr. Durant to wreck again. I feel reasonably confident that the new Board will not allow Mr. Durant to be the dictator of the Company."

Nash would take over the Thomas B. Jeffery Company and begin building Nash automobiles. Storrow tried to get Chrysler to follow Nash out the door. But Durant, using both his salesmanship and a great deal of money, persuaded Chrysler to stay and become president of Buick Motor Company. Chrysler, a strong and talented leader, became an admirer of Durant ("He could charm a bird right down out of a tree," Chrysler once said of his new boss).

But Chrysler quit late in 1919 in a dispute with Durant over control of Buick decisions – though the two remained close friends for life. In the 1920s, Chrysler would take over what was left of Maxwell operations as the basis to form Chrysler Corporation. At Buick, he was succeeded by Harry H. Bassett, who had been president of Charles Stewart Mott's company that had moved to Flint from Utica, N.Y., in 1906-07 to build axles for Buick. When Weston-Mott was absorbed by GM in 1916, Bassett became general manager at Buick under Chrysler's Buick presidency. So he was perfectly positioned to take over for Chrysler. Bassett, though a quiet man whose name is barely remembered compared to his predecessors, was nevertheless an effective leader. Under his direction, the Buick automobile was continually improved until his untimely death at age 51 on October 17, 1926, when he contracted bronchial pneumonia while traveling in France.

Durant, the savior of Buick, Cadillac, Oldsmobile and Oakland (predecessor of Pontiac), the creator of Chevrolet Motor Company, the founder of General Motors and finally its president, was himself removed from power – again – at GM late in 1920 when he became heavily indebted in the stock market. Whether his departure was solely the result of his own stock speculations or a plot by others – or a combination of both – is still debated. Alvan Macauley, president of Packard Motor Car Company, remarked in a letter to U.S. Sen.

The final years

Truman H. Newberry on December 9, 1919: "There is still a clique in Wall Street that hasn't forgiven Durant for his coup in regaining control of General Motors. I have always understood they intend to get him ultimately, and there may be opportunities for them to do so, if things should not continue to break handsomely."

Durant landed on his feet. He promptly created Durant Motors and became the "bull of bulls" in the stock market in the Roaring Twenties.

By the early 1920s, the Buick marque had a solid reputation as one of the world's elite automobiles – in terms of power, reliability, value and style. Beginning about that time, all kinds of leaders were driving Buicks over a 20-year period – from the King of England to the last emperor of China to the sultan of Johore. This was no accident. As Alfred P. Sloan Jr., GM's great leader in the post-Durant era, once commented, Buick succeeded because "it had the management of stars."*

Discussing the state of the business in the early 1920s, Sloan observed: "It was Buick that made any kind of General Motors car worth talking about." In 1921, Sloan wrote to GM Chairman Pierre du Pont: "It is far better that the rest of General Motors be scrapped than any chances taken with Buick's earning power."

By this time, DeWaters had succeeded Marr as chief engineer, though Marr was still working on special projects for the company from his retirement home at Signal Mountain, Tenn. Marr's career had been eventful and rewarding. He helped create Flint's first airplane, the "Flint Flyer," which had a Buick engine, in 1910. He designed an experimental tank for Buick during World War I. Seldom leaving Signal Mountain, he often solved engineering problems sent to

---

* Pu Yi, last emperor of China, was forced to abdicate as a child in 1912 but returned to at least partial power during turbulent political times. Pu Yi bought a six-cylinder Buick on May 8, 1926, from an American agency in Tianjin, according to Wang Qingxiang, a researcher with the Academy of Social Sciences in Jilin Province. He writes in his book, *Extraordinary Citizen,* that Pu Yi took the car, which was painted red, to Changchun and often drove it at the palace there. He even had the national flower of Manchuria painted on the car. Also, Sun Yatsen, first provisional president of the Republic of China, was photographed in a Buick in Shanghai in 1912. A 1941 Buick similar to one owned by the widely respected postwar president of China, Zhou En-Lai, was seen by the writer in a Shanghai museum in 1997.

him from Buick headquarters. His interest in aviation was such that an airfield near Marr's retirement home was named Marr Field. While he didn't like to venture far from his treasured home, he did reminisce about his life in speeches before clubs in Chattanooga and in newspaper interviews during infrequent visits to Flint, where he would visit the Buick plant and such old friends as Charles Stewart Mott. Marr died in 1941.

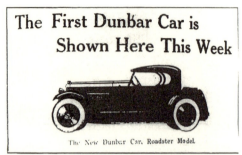

Ad for Dunbar automobile.

Eugene Richard was also still on Buick's payroll and weighing in on engineering decisions until he became ill in 1931. He died in Flint on June 29, 1938.

In June of 1921, David Buick surfaced as president of Lorraine Motors Corporation in Grand Rapids, Mich. The announcement, published in *Automotive Industries,* said David "has designed a new car that will be put on the market shortly." The car would be marketed as the Lorraine but would be different from that which the company had been manufacturing. The new model, it was announced, "will be equipped with a valve-in-head engine, Buick being credited with having brought out the first engine of that type." (George Ferris of Grand Rapids, who once researched and wrote an article on the Lorraine for *Antique Automobile,* told the writer the overhead-valve engine for Lorraine never happened. The Lorraine was powered by an L-head motor.)

Automotive Industries said a "strong organization" had been created. David's associates included A. H. Wyatt, who was "well known in automotive and financial circles in Michigan," and John H. Larkin, former sales manager of the Haynes car of Kokomo, Ind. According to one published report, about 350 Lorraines rolled off the assembly line in the brief period Buick headed the firm before it folded.

The Lorraine car had barely hit the rocks when a story was floated about a new David Buick automobile venture – to build a car named the

The final years

Veteran Buick engine experts Eugene Richard (right) and William Beacraft (next to him) join a future Buick chief engineer, Ferdinand A. (Dutch) Bower, in admiring Buick's one millionth car, a 1923 Model 23-55 Sport Touring. The celebration consisted of a quick photo opportunity on a snowy day near the Flint Buick factory.

Dunbar. *Automobile Topics* for August 12, 1922, reported: "It is understood that negotiations are pending for the purchase of a plant. Production is expected to begin, in five models, early next year. Financial plans are not shown as yet but it is understood that a capital of $5,000,000 will be set upon. The project has been hatching for some little time."

Walden, N.Y., a village of 5,000 people about 85 miles northwest of New York City, was open to such a venture. The local hat factory had just closed, and so had the Borden Company's milk processing plant. That one, a sprawling brick structure dating to 1884 and with 70,000 square feet of floor space, was being peddled by the Dairymen's League. Walden was clearly in the market for some new jobs.

According to Keith Marvin in *Special Interest Autos* in December 1980, the key promoter of the Dunbar car was Harry C. Hoeft, whose top assistant was J. L. Dornbos, vice president and treasurer of the newly formed David Dunbar Buick Corporation, headquartered in New York City.

At a mass meeting in Walden on February 1, 1923, Hoeft outlined the company's plans. The corporation would indeed be capitalized at $5 million. Common stock would be available at $10 a share – or $5 if you were a citizen of Walden. Attractive stock certificates were printed.

Enough money was raised to purchase the former Borden factory, and David Buick himself arrived in Walden on February 15, apparently to oversee the purchase details. On April 26, 1923, *Automotive Industries* confirmed the corporation had bought the plant and said operations were expected to begin in May. Plans now called for building four models of the Dunbar automobile, with the open cars listing for around $1,100 and the closed models at about $1,400.

In August, the corporation opened part of the factory so hundreds of investors and other interested persons could tour the building and see the one Dunbar car, said to have been built for $500 and shipped in from Detroit. A party atmosphere, with picnic tables and refreshments, was created inside the plant.

The car looked good and, with its Continental engine, it ran well. The Walden *Citizen-Herald* said it was painted "in a beautiful maroon with battleship red wheels." The newspaper's editor was given a ride. "The engine works beautifully and the furnishings of the car were first class," it was reported. But when the party was over, the car disappeared, the factory doors closed and nobody even cleaned up. When someone peeked into the building 10 weeks later to see how the factory was progressing, it was discovered, as Marvin wrote, "the site was exactly as it had been when the picnic ended. Plates, napkins and glasses still graced the tables, the room was still festooned with the red, white and blue bunting and the well-fed mice had long since disappeared."

There were only token, futile attempts to sue the backers. Decades later, people were still wondering, though, about whatever happened to that beautiful maroon Dunbar roadster, with its sleek styling and red disc wheels. "I don't think anyone knows where it was built or where it went," Marvin told the writer.

Marvin's story was headlined: "The Dunbar Deception: Was David Buick a schnook or a sharpie?" Interviewed by the writer, Marvin pointed out he didn't write the headline. "David Buick was a bad-luck guy," he said. "He had a series of problems (in his business ventures) after he got out of the plumbing business." Marvin said he

The final years

believes David was ignorant of any fraud plans and was basically "played for a sucker."

By this time in his life, David Buick was now an aging man who had come upon hard times mostly caused by his own poor decisions. He probably jumped too quickly at promotions like the Lorraine and the Dunbar, but he was also desperately poor in an era before the government provided financial safety nets.

The Buick family suffered through years of real poverty. During the rich years, Tom Buick spent $100,000 to improve his $75,000 house in a suburb of Detroit. But his son, David Dunbar Buick II, remembered other times – the family so impoverished it was evicted from 13 apartments for nonpayment of rent. The stress sent his mother to hospitals with migraine headaches before her early death.

As for Tom – the man who had accompanied Walter Marr on the test drive of the first Flint Buick and given Hugh Dolnar the first Buick press ride – he oddly never drove a car in the memory of his son. "It was explained to me that some kid threw a firecracker in our car when I was a baby and dad would not drive again, though I don't know how much stock you can put in that," said David II.

When Tom criticized GM in published interviews for not doing better by his father, his son felt the negative reaction caused him to lose a job as an office boy at GM. David II had landed the job, but was told not to report to work for his first day. David II did once buy a Buick when his name got him on a dealer's preferred list immediately after World War II, when cars were hard to get. He received the car in five days and paid full price.

But eventually David II, grandson of the auto pioneer, got a job in the export department of Chrysler Corporation, where he worked for 25 years before retirement. When the writer interviewed him at his Detroit home in 1980, a Plymouth was in his garage. His only mementos of his grandfather were a few never-published photos (one a profile with a cigar, another with his second wife), a small corroded set of drafting tools (which eventually ended up at Flint's Sloan Museum) and a book of minutes from the David Buick Carburetor Company.

Tom Buick, a small but tough man who David II said had been a

David Buick's Marvelous Motor Car

May-December marriage: David Buick and Margaret Harrington

strike breaker before his Buick Motor Company years, never found a good job after the years with his father's businesses and his brass foundry. He was a Fuller Brush salesman when he died July 4, 1942.

As for David Buick himself, his wife Caroline died in 1916 and he lived with Tom and his family for several years before David's May-December marriage to Margaret Harrington, more than 40 years younger. In 1917, he was producing a carburetor to be manufactured by the Jackson (Mich.) Carburetor Company and in the early '20s, he was president of the above-mentioned David Buick Carburetor Company. Not much was ever heard of them.

Nor was much heard of Buick himself, after the Lorraine and the Dunbar, until 1928, when Bruce Catton found him at the Detroit School of Trades. He and Margaret were living at that time in a flat at 17140 Third Avenue in Detroit.

While Buick was usually upbeat during his conversation with Catton, once he let his guard down. "You know, I've been to practically every one of the friends of the old days – millionaires now, every one – and asked for a job; and none of them had anything for me. I wouldn't want to be president, or treasurer; all I'd want would be security – a feeling that I was all set for the rest of my life. Damn it, I'm not after charity or pity. I'm still strong and able. But you know, it's kind of hard for a man of my age to be uncertain about the future. I've got to have a job."

Catton's article, which included nothing of Buick's business promotions after he left Buick Motor Company, was apparently widely printed. And from it came expressions of sympathy. An engineer in Saskatchewan wrote to Buick in early 1928 that he realized "a man

The final years

of your type craves neither charity or sympathy" but nevertheless offered him "a home and my care at any time you feel that you would like to quit your present vocation and take things easier."

David was disappointed when the 25th anniversary of Buick Motor Company was celebrated in August, 1928, and nobody invited him to the festivities in Flint. But apparently the company under General Manager Ed Strong's leadership was keeping things local. Organizers of the event didn't invite Marr or Durant either.

The Buick family, though lacking in money, was fortunate in one regard – the family was close knit and used to gather in one apartment or another for card games, the grandson recalled. But one night in March of 1929, as the auto pioneer and his wife were about to join a family gathering at son Wynton's house, Margaret called to say he was ill. Tom rushed him to Detroit's Harper Hospital. An operation for a bowel obstruction revealed cancer. Also, the grandson said, the elderly Buick caught pneumonia when a nurse left a window open.

David Buick, 74, died at 8:15 p.m. on March 5, 1929, "leaving only his name on a car," as one newspaper article phrased it. Surviving besides his second wife Margaret were his sons, Thomas D. and Wynton R., daughters, Mrs. James (Mabel Lucille) Coyle of Detroit and Mrs. Frank C. (Frances Jane) Patterson of Los Angeles, and a half-sister, Mrs. J. Kutz, also of Detroit. Services were at the Henry J. Hastings funeral rooms. Burial was in Woodmere Cemetery in Detroit. The standup tombstone is engraved with a Buick script.

His obituary was widely published. Some of the articles, such as the following, were severe:

> Mr. Buick, whose name appears on the gleaming front of approximately 2,000,000 automobiles, died a penniless, forlorn, bitterly disappointed man. For years he lived and worked in the very shadow of the wing of fortune. At his finger tips danced millions. Around the corner waited uncounted and almost unaccountable wealth. Time after time he saw the doors of Midas swinging before him, but always, just before he could enter these golden realms, they swung shut in his face and left him on the outside, bewildered, puzzled, disappointed.

David Buick's Marvelous Motor Car

With that kind of publicity, inevitably letters arrived at Buick headquarters wondering why the founder and namesake had been allowed to die in poverty.

A doctor in New Jersey wrote: "Countless thousands have read with horror and disgust of the distressing circumstances attending the death of David D. Buick…the reaction of the general public against the Buick Company is most unfavorable."

A man in Cleveland observed "the passing of David Buick appears to be a pretty sad affair…I have been the proud owner of six Buick cars, but I do not feel quite so proud this morning…We pension the old soldiers, and have homes for the indigent, but David Buick, founder of the company which builds the magnificent car bearing his name, has to die in poverty."

A man in Grand Rapids, Mich., offered to be the first to contribute "a small sum of money" to erect a monument in David Buick's memory. From Pinehurst, Ga., came a suggestion that the company set aside $1 for each Buick sold "during the present year if not longer" for a fund for Buick's family.

In some cases, Ed Strong, the general manager, sent dealers and others to visit the writers and try to explain the company's relationship with its founder. The facts were that David Buick had left on his own, had been given a substantial amount of money on his departure, and had been gone for 20 years. And for those who still doubted, the Buick firm could point to a *Time* magazine article of March 18, 1929, that basically put most of the blame for David's plight on the man himself.

The company might have pointed out that upon arriving in the California oil fields after leaving Buick Motor Company, David had described himself as "a very rich man," even if that was an overstatement. The founder's later financial problems were of his own making, an opinion David Buick never denied. As *Time* pointed out: "He left the company with a block of stock which would soon have made him an exceedingly rich man. But David Buick seemed to have no affinity for money. He could not make it himself and he was not content to let abler business men make it for him."

Certainly Buick was not alone in running into hard times – the

The final years

Great Depression would soon put many others in similar circumstances. Indeed, at the time of Buick's death, GM founder Billy Durant himself was only a few years from bankruptcy (though Durant did get financial help in his later years from the personal funds of old associates Walter Chrysler, Alfred P. Sloan Jr. and Charles Stewart Mott. Durant was operating a bowling alley in Flint a few years before his death in New York on March 18, 1947).

David Buick II once wrote to Sloan, asking if he had any information regarding his grandfather's departure from Buick. "He sent back a hand-written note saying he had no recollection – it had all happened before his time," the grandson recalled.

But not all connections between the Buick family and former colleagues were severed. David II remembered that years later Billy Durant sometimes came to his father's house for Sunday dinner and once gave the boy a beautiful blank diary.

Almost a decade passed after David's death. And then GM began to resurrect his name. The corporation's design staff wanted to use the Buick family coat of arms to decorate the front of automobiles. That inevitably would bring attention to the man. The name had already adorned more than 2 million vehicles (by the time of the Buick company's centennial, the count had reached nearly 37 million).

The Buick crest debuted as an emblem on the nose of 1937 Buicks. The icon was based on a reference found by GM designer Ralph Pew in the 1851 edition of *Burke's Heraldry* he found in the Detroit Public Library (for an unknown reason the reference was dropped in later editions).

As Howard E. O'Leary, assistant director of GM's Styling Section, wrote to Buick Manufacturing Manager Edward T. Ragsdale on September 23, 1937: "Back in 1935 and 1936, the idea of using the Buick crest was thought of by Mr. Earl (Harley Earl, GM's first and legendary design chief) and the writer. We discussed it many times." He discussed sending Pew to the library in search of a Buick crest.

"I might add that our thinking of using the Buick crest was an outgrowth of the fact that it has been a custom on automobiles, where the name of the car is the name of a family, to employ the crest if

David Buick's Marvelous Motor Car

David Buick in 1928, at the time he was interviewed by Bruce Catton.

one exists," O'Leary wrote. "I am only adding this so that you will not get the mistaken idea that we had an idea in the Styling Section, as they are coming so damn few and far between I would hate to mislead you."

The coat of arms was a red shield with a checkered silver and azure diagonal line running from the upper left corner to the lower right, an antlered deer head with a jagged ("erazed") neckline in the upper right section of the shield and a gold cross in the shield's lower left section, the cross pierced in the center. It's likely David Buick had never seen nor heard of it.

Today, it's greatly changed, with three shields instead of one (starting in 1960 to symbolize the LeSabre, Invicta and Electra models introduced for '59). The details have been removed for clarity and the colors dropped for what marketing folks call "edge." The so-called "tri-shield" logo decorates the grilles of Buick cars and trucks more than 100 years after incorporation. (Buick crest photos, page 204).

Very subtly, the man is still part of the car.

Even so, David Buick's identity seemed to slide further into the darkness. In 1968, Beverly Rae Kimes in *Automobile Quarterly* quoted an unnamed contemporary: "Fame beckoned to David Buick – he sipped from the cup of greatness…and then spilled what it held." Kimes observed: "Seldom has history produced such an unrecalled – or misrecalled – man."

Or, maybe not.

When the *Glasgow Sunday Post* in Scotland noted on September 15, 1974, that the 120th anniversary of David Buick's birth was that

The final years

week, the headline read "But who remembers David Buick?" The clipping arrived in the mail of Buick General Manager George Elges, who replied: "I would like to answer your question, 'Who remembers David Buick?' We do – all 18,000 of us employed here at Buick, plus a community of some 200,000 people in Flint, 3,200 Buick dealers in the United States, not to mention the 5 ½ million around the world still driving Buicks."

Elges, whose letter was probably ghost-written by Buick PR Director Jerry Rideout, noted "it just so happens that yesterday (September 26, 1974), a new highway was opened here and dedicated to your Scotland native. The new Buick Freeway now provides a faster and more convenient link between the Motor City, which is Detroit, and Buick town, which is Flint."

Unfortunately, that wasn't true for long. A state legislator, to the chagrin of the United Auto Workers official he was trying to impress, persuaded the Legislature to change the name of the expressway to the UAW Freeway. Then the state renamed another local freeway, which was to have honored Louis Chevrolet, as the Chevrolet-Buick Freeway on a small sign. Buick couldn't even get top billing on a freeway in Flint. Not only that, one of the homes of James Whiting, the man who had brought Buick to Flint, was razed to make way for the Buick (now UAW) Freeway.

But there was other recognition. In 1976, volunteers at the Sloan Museum, working with the museum's Jim Johnson, recreated the original Flint Buick that David Buick and Walter Marr had built in the summer of 1904 – a U.S. Bicentennial local history project. The replica of that first Flint Buick, looking as it did in the summer of 1904 when it had no body, no fenders, was made more authentic by being fitted with one of two existing 1904 Buick engines. The idea came from Charles Hulse with major support from the museum's director, Roger Van Bolt, and Buick enthusiasts G. Gregory Fauth and Jack Skaff.

Johnson, his father, Gerald, and the volunteers drove it to Detroit and back, just like in 1904. They stopped for lunch with the news media at the Detroit Press Club, which was coincidentally on Howard Street, where Buick Manufacturing Company and then Buick Motor

David Buick's Marvelous Motor Car

Company had operated before the move to Flint. The next morning they left the GM Building for the return to Flint, retracing the original route through Lapeer.

The trip took 12 minutes longer in July of 1976 than in 1904. Various problems with fuel, spark plugs and even cotter pins created some difficult moments. The writer remembers helping push the car through the turn at Lapeer. But the trip ended triumphantly before a small crowd on E. First Street near Saginaw Street, where the original car was photographed in 1904. (The replica, usually displayed at Flint's Sloan Museum, was being rebuilt in 2006).

In 1994, at Buick's World Headquarters building in Flint, the company unveiled a Michigan historical marker, a beautiful sign with brass words on a green background, describing David Buick's career, the Flint complex and the beginnings of General Motors. Within a dozen years, though, the headquarters staff had moved to Detroit, the impressive white marble and glass administration building – that opened in 1968 – had been razed, and hundreds of acres of bleak, vacant land were visible on the site of Buick City, the storied Buick home plant. No factories, not even scrub oak as in 1905 – just flat bare clay. Oh, and the historical marker had disappeared.

In his late 80s, retired Buick PR Director Jerry Rideout was stirred by the announcement of plans to raze the plant to fire off a letter to *The Flint Journal.* This "hallowed plot of land," he bitterly observed, had been the home of Buick for nearly all of the 20th century and had "housed the cornerstone upon which Billy Durant founded General Motors in 1908." Said Rideout: "It was the product of this site that put the city of Flint on the global map. Now it is to be razed, to become just a plot of land in a city already overrun with vacant lots."

However, in 2004, in time for the 150th anniversary of David's birth, another state marker was displayed at GM World Headquarters at Detroit's Renaissance Center. It pointed out David Buick's first engine shop, Buick Auto-Vim and Power Company, had been located just a few blocks up the street (Beaubien) and that his fledgling auto company, after the move to Flint, eventually became the financial foundation for GM's birth.

Commemorating David Buick's birthplace in Arbroath, Scotland, on June 9, 1994, are (from left) Eric Buick of Arbroath (no relation); Bob Coletta, Buick general sales and service manager (and later general manager); Larry Gustin of Buick PR, who with Eric arranged for the plaque, and Brian Milne, who as head of the Angus District Council was Arbroath's top elected official.

A decade earlier, in June of 1994, when Buick officials journeyed to Arbroath, Scotland, to unveil a plaque at his birthplace, the gesture played in newspapers throughout Great Britain, and especially in Scotland, as well as in the United States. The BBC even sent a television news crew to Flint to retell the story of the Scotsman who had such an impact on the industry. The feature was telecast in 23 countries.

At the unveiling of the plaque, on the only building left on Green Street in Arbroath, Robert E. Coletta, Buick's general sales manager and soon-to-be general manager, paid this tribute: "Buick has been one of the great names in American automobiles through virtually all of the 20th century. It is certainly appropriate for us to honor this man, not only because his name identifies our automobiles, but because his genius and hard work formed the beginning of an unsurpassed automotive success story – that is still being written."

Those words were heard first hand by this writer, who introduced Coletta to the gathering on that brisk morning in Arbroath. The scene included five vintage Buick cars (1939 to mid '50s) driven by individual owners who had heard of the planned event, and a new model

David Buick's Marvelous Motor Car

Buick Park Avenue brought in from Europe to transport Coletta's party to the plaque site. Also a speaker was Arbroath native Eric Buick who had worked with company officials to create the plaque. Another man witnessing the ceremony was named David Buick. The speakers, including the writer, made the point that while David Buick was ultimately not financially successful, his name by that time had appeared on more than 32 million automobiles – including 9 million still on the road. About a half million Buicks a year were being built. "How many of us," the audience was asked, "would like that kind of legacy?"

A letter to the mayor of Flint read by Brian Milne, Arbroath's top political leader as provost of the Angus District Council, said "the bonds of kinship and friendship between our two countries are very strong and the link between Arbroath and Flint through David Dunbar Buick strengthens these bonds in a more personal way."

The Buick centennial was celebrated in 2003, an occasion for many stories to be told about the founder and his company. As a centennial event, Buick developed a touring heritage exhibit of vintage cars, photos and other artifacts and sent it to selected museums across the country, hosting press events and VIP receptions in Los Angeles, Reno, St. Louis, Saratoga Springs, Detroit and Flint.

A giant celebration in Flint combined with the Buick Club of America's national meet, orchestrated by Dennis Meyer of the club's Flint "Buicktown" chapter, attracted an impressive 1,800 vintage Buicks. Nicola Bulgari, international jeweler and probably the world's leading collector of vintage Buicks, brought 10 of his cars to the event. He also donated full-size and model cars to the Buick Gallery and Research Center, which had been dedicated November 10, 1998, as a subsidiary of the Sloan Museum in Flint.

As a centennial project, Buick Motor Division, the Buick Club of America and the club's Buicktown chapter funded restoration of a 1905 Model C that had been in Flint longer than any other Buick – 100 years. Charles Hulse left a handwritten note that said it was built April 17, 1905. The source of that information is unknown, but he may well have seen the first production records, which disappeared after the early 1950s. If that date is correct, the car would likely be the

The final years

oldest or second oldest existing Buick, but its engine number (3076) would appear to make it the seventh oldest in existence. (The car believed to be the oldest Buick, in Harold Warp's Pioneer Village in Minden, Neb., was said to have probably been built in April of 1905, but nobody knows if the engines were installed in order by engine number, or even if they were later replaced). The Flint car had been rescued years earlier from the garage of Fred A. Aldrich, onetime Durant-Dort Carriage Company secretary. It had been purchased new for $950 by Aldrich – the man who helped James Whiting summon Billy Durant to Flint on the trip that led to Durant's takeover of Buick.

On September 17, 2004, the 150th anniversary of David Buick's birth, Eric Buick hosted a luncheon for local officials at Buick's birthplace in Arbroath, Scotland. In Birmingham, Mich., the founder was recognized at a dinner tied to the Ryder Cup and Buick's involvement with golf, with miniatures of the Buick state historical marker decorating tables. In Detroit, David Buick was remembered with a toast at that marker, newly erected outside GM headquarters.

In Flint, which was Buick Motor Division's headquarters for 95 years, the Sloan Museum and Buick Gallery were opened free of charge that weekend by Director Tim Shickles. The city still celebrates its storied past with the restored Durant-Dort Carriage Company headquarters, today a national historic landmark; the restored home of Charles W. Nash in his Durant-Dort days; the restored Flint Road Cart Company plant; statues of Durant and Dort; Charles Stewart Mott's home; the Sloan Museum and its Buick Gallery and Research Center; and the return of downtown Flint's famed arches from the early 20th century – including one sponsored by Buick Motor Division after the division's headquarters had been moved from Flint to Detroit. At nearby Historical Crossroads Village, a small horse barn that had once belonged to Durant is on display. It came from the property of Durant's Flint home (and was identified as a Durant building by its onetime owner, Ernest Gardner).

David Buick was named to the Automotive Hall of Fame now in Dearborn, Mich., in January 1974. Durant is there as well, but the Buick name is certainly more widely recognized, thanks to the name on the product. It's fair to suggest David would be pleased.

"Success is mostly hard work," Buick had told Bruce Catton during that 1928 interview. "It's work and it's stick-to-it-ive-ness... I'm not worrying. The failure is the man who stays down when he falls – the man who sits and worries about what happened yesterday instead of jumping up and figuring what he's going to do today and tomorrow. That's what success is –looking ahead to tomorrow." The reporter noted a sign on Buick's desk: "No trials, no triumphs."

Catton was impressed. Summing up his interview with the man, he came to the conclusion David Buick was a heroic figure. Catton's impression: "This man, whose name is world famous, but whose purse is thin, is neither discouraged nor unhappy...His eyes, that have seen the company he founded go on to greatness without him, are bright and cheerful. He does not seem defeated.

"The giants of the automobile world are true giants, that cannot be crushed; and David Buick, if you will, is one of them."

Giant? Maybe not. Maybe you reserve that word for Durant and Ford and a very few others. When the Society of Automotive Historians created a list of the industry's 30 most significant figures, it ranked Henry Ford No. 1, Billy Durant No. 2 and Walter Chrysler No. 3. Charles W. Nash placed 10th. Three one-time Buick people had made the top-10 list – but David Buick didn't make the top 30.

But certainly you could credit David Buick for tenacity. Coming out of the 19th century with little more than an idea of how to build gasoline engines, he attracted such brilliant mechanical minds as Walter Marr and then Eugene Richard, presided over the development of superior engines, found just enough money to stay afloat and held his tiny company together long enough to get the Buick automobile into production.

It took others – Durant and his associates – to make the Buick marque great, and to use it to create General Motors. But David Buick set the stage, from before the turn of the century to 1905. Marr and Richard and others wandered in and out of the spotlight, but only one was always there, David Buick, chasing a dream that he could build a motor car.

Lawrence R. Gustin

Boydell Building (foreground), still standing at Beaubien and Lafayette (previously Champlain) in downtown Detroit, housed Buick Auto-Vim and Power Company in 1900. The building today is within sight of Buick Motor Division's marketing headquarters in Renaissance Center (background), which is also General Motors headquarters.

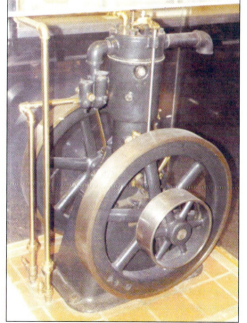

This overhead-valve 4-horsepower stationary engine in the Smithsonian Institution was built in Detroit by Buick Manufacturing Company, predecessor of Buick Motor Company, and is likely the oldest surviving engine produced by one of David Buick's companies. It was probably built in 1903.

Ron DeGraw

Ron DeGraw

From the Marr family collection: Above, portraits of Abbie and Walter Marr in retirement in 1930s at 'Marrcrest' at Signal Mountain, Tenn. The rest are photos of the 1903 Marr Autocar, a link between the first Buick completed in 1900 or 1901 by Walter Marr, and the 1904 Buicks he returned to build. Below (left) are Marr's great grandson, Barton Close, and his wife, Cindy, and (right) Bill and Sarah Close at Amelia Island Concours d' Elegance after winning best-in-class trophy. Sarah is a granddaughter of Walter and Abbie Marr.

First Flint Buick is being completed at the factory on W. Kearsley in June or early July of 1904 in this fine illustration by an unidentified artist. It was used for the cover of a Buick Motor Division brochure produced in honor of Buick's 75th anniversary in 1978.

1910 Model 10

1910 Model 16 Roadster

Buick

No automobile manufacturer in existence today can claim a more prestigious heritage than Buick Motor Division, which is celebrating its 75th anniversary in 1978.

Few manufacturers can claim more industry firsts that are almost universal today — the valve-in-head engine, directional signals, tinted glass, the torque converter transmission, all were pioneered by Buick.

Certainly no manufacturer can claim such a distinguished list of industry giants as were spawned by Buick: William C. Durant, the founder of General Motors; Walter P. Chrysler, founder of Chrysler Corporation; Charles W. Nash, founder of Nash Motor Company (now American Motors); Louis Chevrolet, who made his name as a race driver for Buick; and Harlow H. Curtice, who later became president of General Motors — all were products of Buick Motor Division and are a part of its proud heritage.

While the Buick heritage rests principally on its record as a manufacturer of premier automobiles, in its 75 years it also has built an enviable reputation for the production of a wide variety of military hardware in two World Wars.

It all began in 1903 — September 10th to be exact — when a group of Flint businessmen, headed by James H. Whiting, borrowed $10,000 from a local bank and bought the financially-troubled Buick Motor Company and brought it to Flint.

This was probably the most important single loan in the community's history, since it not only brought Buick to Flint, but subsequently the extensive General Motors operations which provided some 75,000 jobs in the area.

David Dunbar Buick, the man who lent his name to it all, was an obscure Detroit plumber and inventor before he turned his talents to the automobile business.

We don't know as much about the man as we'd like to. We know his parents brought him to America two years after his birth in Scotland in 1854. More than 80 years later, when Buick

Terry B. Dunham

(Above) Buick Manufacturing Company catalog, circa 1902. (Right) Rare 1904 Buick stationary engine.

Replica of the first Flint Buick is shown here on E. First Street in Flint, at the site where the original was first photographed in 1904. The replica, which has an original 1904 Buick motor, is positioned with last Buick built in Flint – the last car off the Buick City assembly line June 29, 1999 – a 1999 Buick LeSabre, which Buick donated to the Sloan Museum.

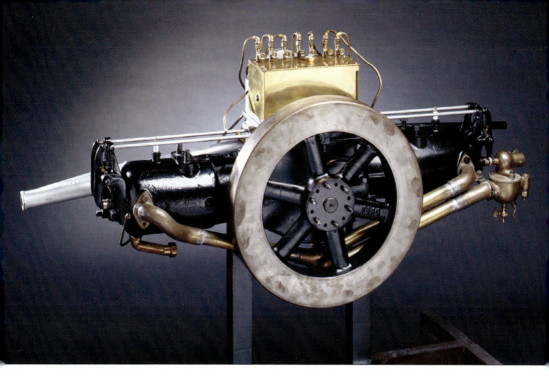

Above: A 1905 Model C valve-in-head two-cylinder automobile engine, from Fred Aldrich's car that was restored as a centennial project. Below: A 1905 Model C, the first Buick to go into serious production. Of about 750 Buicks built that year, 14 are known to exist. This one, owned for decades by early West Coast Buick dealer and distributor Charles Howard (later famous as the owner of the great race horse Seabiscuit), is believed to be the first Buick sold on the West Coast.

Downtown Flint about the time Buick arrived.

Flint Wagon Works, whose directors bought Buick Motor Company and brought it to Flint.

In 1905, Buick took over this plant in Jackson, Mich., for assembly.

Lineup of 1905 Model C Buicks in downtown Jackson, Mich., after production was moved from Flint to Jackson in early 1905.

Early views of north Flint complex via colorized postcards.

More colorized postcards of Buick's north Flint complex.

Buick headquarters offices at north Flint complex.

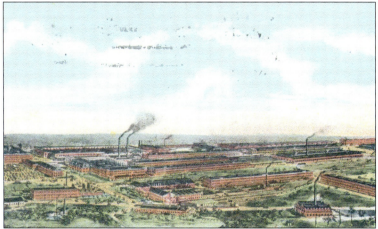

Early Buick racer on track in New Jersey (top); the complete Buick complex in north Flint (center); shipping day around 1910 (bottom left).

Top: Dresden Hotel in downtown Flint where W.C. Durant met Ben Briscoe in 1908 to start talks that eventually led to the creation of General Motors. Right: Buick's second Administration Building, opened in 1917. Below: Buick home complex in late 1960s, with the third Administration Building (at bottom) just completed.

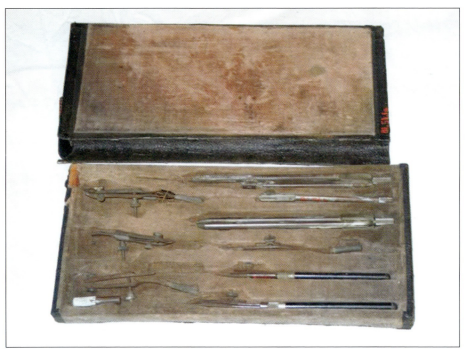

One of the few surviving personal artifacts of David Buick is his drafting set, donated by his grandson, David Dunbar Buick II, to the Buick Gallery and Research Center of the Sloan Museum in Flint.

Walter Marr's experimental Cyclecar, circa 1915, with his grandchildren (from left) Anne Ballard, Sarah Close, Joan Williams, Richard Marr and Walter (Skip) Marr III.

David Buick's great-grandson, Doug Boes, displays a small brass cannon used by David Buick to start regattas in Detroit, back before he became an automotive pioneer.

1913 Logo

1920 Service Sign

1942 Crest

1947 Crest

1959 Tri-Shield

1990 Tri-Shield

Celebrating Buick heritage: Top, a gathering views the unveiling of a plaque at David Buick's birthplace in Arbroath, Scotland, in June 1994. Above, Bob Coletta, Buick general sales and service manager, and Brian Milne, Arbroath's top elected official, with vintage Buicks and the plaque on the building at the birthplace site. Below left, Coletta, Buick PR Director Jack DeCou and Buick General Manager Ed Mertz unveil a state historical marker in Flint in 1994. Below right, the marker at GM Headquarters in Detroit, created in connection with Buick's 100th anniversary in 2003 and installed in 2004 in time for the 150th anniversary of David Buick's birth. The marker is on Jefferson at Beaubien in downtown Detroit, a few blocks from the original site of Buick Auto-Vim and Power Company.

Buick's centennial celebration in Flint in July of 2003. Top row, from left: Harold Calhoun's truck that transported the Buick Blackhawk show car was a traveling centennial ad; closeup of David Buick's family crest on Blackhawk, a highly stylized car based on a 1939 design. Second row: Early Buicks on display; Buick history enthusiast Greg Fauth with his 1911 Model 26 Runabout. Third row: A lineup of Buick Reatta two-seaters (1988-91); Buicks from the late '40s and early '50s with portholes and carnivorous grilles. About 1,800 vintage Buicks were displayed.

Below, Nicola Bulgari, international jeweler and vintage Buick collector, visits statues of Durant and Dort and is interviewed while sitting in one of his cars at the centennial event.

Above: Buick World Headquarters in Flint, just before the move to Detroit in 1998. By 2006, the building had been demolished, along with most of the huge factory complex. Below, Buick marketing's new home at GM headquarters in Renaissance Center in downtown Detroit – several blocks from original site of Buick Auto-Vim and Power Company.

Preserving the past, promoting the future – Above: Inside the Buick Gallery and Research Center at Flint's Sloan Museum. In the photo at top, the replica of the first Flint Buick of 1904 is in the foreground, the Buick Bug racer of 1910 is in the background. Above, the Buick concept XP-300 of 1951 is in the foreground at the Buick Gallery. Below: GM Vice Chairman Robert A. Lutz introduces the 2005 Buick LaCrosse to the news media at Bay Harbor, Michigan. LaCrosse is displayed with a 1905 Model C from David Buick's time of 100 years earlier, and a 50th anniversary Buick, the classic 1953 Skylark.

Acknowledgments

Terry B. Dunham, my co-author of *The Buick: A Complete History* in six editions (1980-2002), including five revised and updated, is specifically thanked for sharing information and opinions, and for commenting at length on numerous drafts of this work. Terry's enthusiasm, his personal contributions and the historical materials from his files have improved it immeasurably. Without his encouragement, this book would not have been attempted. Many thanks are also due William B. Close, husband of Walter Marr's granddaughter, Sarah. Bill Close has carefully studied the early years of Walter Marr's career. He even bought and completely restored the only existing Marr Autocar – which is a link to the first Buick automobile ever built. Bill has offered information and his own fascinating thoughts on those pioneering days when David Buick and Walter Marr were creating the early history of the Buick automobile, and has filled in many of the blanks in this barely documented period.

The late Charles E. Hulse also deserves many thanks from all of those interested in the early history of Buick and of Flint (and of Oldsmobile, as well). Hulse was personally helpful to me, and assured that after his death all of his research on Buick's early years would be preserved. The Hulse collection includes notes on his personal interviews with Walter Marr and many others and on the news articles he discovered by spending countless hours looking through microfilms of early newspapers. Hulse's Buick material is now available at the Sloan Museum's Buick Gallery and Research Center in Flint, the gift of his daughter, Susan Kelley. For original material on William C. Durant, appreciation goes to the late Catherine L. Durant, his widow; Aristo Scrobogna, who was Durant's last personal secretary; and Scrobogna's daughter, Estelle Roberts, who preserved and gave me Durant's personal letters and other documents, including drafts of his unfinished autobiography.

David Buick's Marvelous Motor Car

Kevin M. Kirbitz, who is helping create a new generation of Buick automobiles as a General Motors engineer, provided key pieces of information, as well as a thorough explanation of the workings of the valve-in-head engine. Kevin generously offered the separate article on overhead-valve engines used in this volume. Kevin is among the best of a young new group of enthusiastic Buick historians. Another fine young Buick historian, Don Bent, whose excellent 2005 book, *A Place Called Buick,* describes in words and pictures the size and colorful history of the Buick home plant in Flint, helped in preparing photos for publication.

In Arbroath, Scotland, where David Buick was born, another man with the Buick name, Eric Buick (no relation), shared information on the village and on Buick genealogy – and he and his wife Amy provided gracious hospitality to my wife Rose Mary and me on the occasion of our visit to Arbroath in 1994. Another resource was Michael Dixon, a student of early Detroit engine and marine history, who provided several specific pieces of information on David Buick's life, including facts about his involvement with sailboating and powerboats. At the Sloan Museum and its Buick Gallery and Research Center in Flint, Mich., Director Tim Shickles and Assistant Director Jeff Taylor enthusiastically supported the research effort. Leroy Cole, former president of the Society of Automotive Historians, kindly opened up his vast collection of automotive books, documents and other papers and photographs and was always available with guidance and encouragement. Michael W. R. Davis, a veteran of automotive journalism and auto public relations, kindly offered access to his unpublished master's thesis on one of the early industry's mysterious figures, Charles G. Annesley. In Flint, Greg Fauth, Jack Skaff, Jim Johnson and David White, along with the late Roger Van Bolt, Clarence H. Young, Richard P. Scharchburg and Merle Perry, were always helpful with advice and information. All of them shared an appreciation for the auto pioneers and the dramatic events they created in the Vehicle City. For information on the Wilkinson and Franklin cars, both of which featured overhead-valve engines, thanks to Frank Hantak, trustee and treasurer of the Franklin Auto-

Acknowledgments

mobile Museum in Tucson, Arizona. For information on the Marmon automobile, which also featured overhead-valve engines, thanks to Chic Kleptz of Dayton, Ohio, who owns more than 20 Marmons. For information which resulted in saving Billy Durant's horse barn, thanks to Ernest Gardner and his daughter, my childhood friend Janet. Several of the photographs of early Buicks in this book were taken over several years by David Franklin, an exceptionally talented automobile photographer.

During many years of research on Buick history (covering more than four decades), I interviewed several people who had personally known David Buick, all of whom have since died: His grandson, David Dunbar Buick II; Fred G. Hoelzle, a longtime Buick employee who knew David Buick as early as 1904; Charles Stewart Mott, a 60-year member of the GM board of directors; and the above-mentioned Catherine L. Durant. Also helpful have been members of Walter Marr's family, including grandsons Walter L. Marr III and Richard A. Marr, the previously mentioned granddaughter Sarah (Mathes) Close and her husband, William B., and Dan N. Williams, husband of another Marr granddaughter, Joan (Hays); and also Eugene C. Richard's son, Eugene D. Richard. An important source for anyone writing about Flint's early industrial development is Frank M. Rodolf's manuscript, "An Industrial History of Flint," in the editorial library of *The Flint Journal,* where he worked in the 1930s and early 1940s. On an evening in New York in 1972, after a meeting with Catherine Durant, I discussed with Rodolf his personal interviews of Billy Durant in the days when Durant owned a Flint bowling establishment near the Buick complex he had created decades earlier. George S. May, author of *A Most Unique Machine,* was also helpful with advice on Buick history in the early 1970s.

George H. Maines, a widely known personality in Flint who handled public relations for such national figures as Hucy Long and numerous entertainment and sports stars, spent hours talking about Flint pioneer automotive figures he had known from his childhood. "In the early days of this (the 20th) century, Flint had a group of men of unusual ability," he once told me. "There was probably not a more lively bunch anywhere else in the country. And the spark plug of them all was Billy Durant." Maines, whose father was a business associate of Durant's, was among a number of people who lived in Flint during the 1950s and '60s who helped bring to life the almost-forgotten days when Buick, Chevrolet and General Motors were created. Thanks also to Tom Klug, associate professor of history at Marygrove College, Detroit, for the reference to C.B. Calder of the Detroit Shipbuilding Company, and to Michael Dixon for pointing out its significance. Kim Crawford of *The Flint Journal,* who has written a fine and detailed book-length manuscript about the life of Jacob Smith, the fur trader who founded the Flint settlement, helped in checking Flint facts. Bob Gritzinger, now an editor at *AutoWeek,* helped me research information for Buick's state historical marker in Detroit. Auto writers Don Sherman and Dan McCosh also provided advice on auto-engine history and technology. In trying to flesh out David Buick's years in California and the legal battles of Buick Oil Company, researcher George J. Fogelson of Redondo Beach, Calif., was particularly helpful, as was Gwen Patterson in finding records at the National Archives and Records Administration in Laguna Niguel, Calif.

Among those who were kind enough to read drafts of this manuscript and offer advice were Charles K. Hyde, professor of history at Wayne State University; David L. Lewis, professor of business history at the University of Michigan; two former Buick PR directors, Jack DeCou and Margaret G. Holmes; Mark Patrick, curator of the National Automotive History Collection at the Detroit Public Library; and Roger Van Noord, retired managing editor of *The Flint Journal* and biographer of the Beaver Island (Michigan) Mormon king, James Jesse Strang. Also, special thanks to Phil Nanzetta and Jeremy Brenn of Signature Book Printing for their creativity, attention to detail and hard work in the production of this book.

David Buick had two sons, Thomas D. and Wynton R., and two daughters, Frances Jane (Mrs. Frank Patterson) of Los Angeles and Mabel Lucille (Mrs. James Coyle) of Detroit. I interviewed David Dunbar Buick II, Thomas's son, who has since died, and Doug Boes, who is the

Acknowledgments

adopted grandson of Frances Jane Patterson. Frances's daughter, Caroline, married Warren Boes. Others interviewed include Sally Buick of Birmingham, Mich., and William Walcott Buick of Bryn Athyn, Pa. William said his grandfather, Detroiter William Dunbar Buick, was a "first cousin, twice removed" of David Dunbar Buick. Sally's late husband, Henry Wolcott Buick, was William's brother. Sally has two sons, Jeffrey and David Dunbar Buick.

Finally, I want to thank my wife Rose Mary, our sons Robert L. Gustin and David M. Gustin and their families, and my late parents Robert S. and Doris M. Gustin, for their support over a number of years of research on Buick Motor Division and its personalities. My paternal grandfather, Edward M. Gustin, had worked for the Durant-Dort Carriage Company around 1899 before becoming an executive at Flint Motor Axle Company on the Buick complex's Flint site, and my mother's father, Thomas E. Irving, moved to Flint with his family from Barrow-in-Furness, England, in 1928 to work at Buick, from which he retired as a wood patternmaker in 1952.

BOOKS

Solid and original information on David Buick is found in only a few automotive history books. The most informative for this effort were *A Most Unique Machine* by George S. May, *The Turning Wheel* by Arthur Pound, and *My Father* by Margery Durant. Several Henry Ford biographies were also helpful. Allen Nevins' *Ford: The Times, The Man, The Company,* and Sidney Olson's delightful *Young Henry Ford* were particularly useful because they best described the times and the people in Detroit at the very time David Buick and Walter Marr were trying to perfect automobiles, although they rarely if ever mention Buick or Marr.

Bent, Don, *A Place Called Buick,* Flint, Mich.: Bent, 2005.

Crow, Carl, *The City of Flint Grows Up,* New York: Harper, 1945.

Curcio, Andrew, *Chrysler: The Life and Times of an Automotive Genius,* Oxford University Press, 2000.

Dammann, George H., *Seventy Years of Buick,* Glen Ellyn, Illinois: Crestline, 1973.

Dixon, Michael M., *Motormen and Yachting: Waterfront Heritage of the Automobile Industry,* Detroit, Mervue Publications (www.mervuepublications.com), 2005.

Dunham, Terry B. and Gustin, Lawrence R., *The Buick: A Complete History,* sixth (Centennial) edition, Automobile Quarterly, 2002.

Durant, Margery, *My Father,* New York: Knickerbocker Press, 1929.

Glasscock, G.C, *The Gasoline Age,* Indianapolis and New York: Bobbs-Merrill, 1937.

Gustin, Lawrence R., *Billy Durant, Creator of General Motors,* Grand Rapids: Eerdmans, 1973. Second edition, Flushing, Mich.: Craneshaw publishers, 1984.

Gustin, Lawrence R., editor, *The Flint Journal Centennial Picture History of Flint,* Flint, Mich.: The Flint Journal, revised third edition, 1977.

Hyde, Charles K., *The Dodge Brothers: The Men, The Motor Cars, and the Legacy,* Detroit: Wayne State University Press, 2005.

Lacey, Robert, *Ford: The Men and the Machine,* Boston-Toronto: Little, Brown, 1986.

Lewis, David L., *The Public Image of Henry Ford: An American Folk Hero and His Company,* Detroit: Wayne State University Press, 1976.

Maines, George H., *Men, A City, and Buick,* pamphlet, Flint, Michigan: Advertisers Press, 1953.

May, George S., *A Most Unique Machine: The Michigan Origins of the American Automobile Industry,* Grand Rapids, Mich.: Eerdmans, 1975.

May, George S., *R.E. Olds: Auto Industry Pioneer,* Grand Rapids, Mich: Eerdmans, 1977

Nevins, Allen, *Ford: The Times, The Man, The Company,* New York: Charles Scribner's Sons, 1954.

Olson, Sidney, *Young Henry Ford,* Detroit: Wayne State University Press, 1963.

Pound, Arthur, *The Turning Wheel, The Story of General Motors Through 25 Years,* Garden City, N.Y.: Doubleday, Doran, 1934.

Seltzer, Lawrence H., *A Financial History of the American Automobile Industry,* Boston and New York: Riverside Press Cambridge, 1928.

Sloan, Alfred P. Jr., with Boyden Sparks, *Adventure of a White Collar Man,* New York: Doubleday, Doran, 1941.

Sloan, Alfred P. Jr., *My Years With General Motors,* New York: Doubleday, 1964.

Therou, Francois, *Buick "The Golden Era" 1903-1915,* Brea, Calif.: Decir, 1971, primarily early catalog reprints.

ARTICLES

This is a partial list of newspaper and magazine articles that were helpful.

The Detroit Tribune, September 4, 1899, *Local Automobile Makers Busily Hustling Things.* Small story with important message about Walter Marr's tricycle engine and his relationship with Charles G. Annesley.

Buick Manufacturing Company, catalog, Terry B. Dunham Collection.

The Automobile and Motor Review, December 20, 1902, a brief account of Marr Auto Car Company being formed.

The Motor World, May 21, 1903, on Buick Motor Company incorporation.

The Motor World, September 29, 1903, on Buick moving to Flint.

Cycle and Automobile Trade Journal, October 1903, Hugh Dolnar, *The Marr Autocar.*

Buick Motor Company, catalog, 1904, Terry B. Dunham Collection. Copy in Buick Gallery and Research Center, Sloan Museum, Flint.

Cycle and Automobile Trade Journal, March 1904, Buick ad; November and December 1904, Buick car ads.

The Automobile, July 30, 1904, discusses first drive (Detroit-Flint-Detroit July 9-12).

Automobile Review, September 10, 1904, *Buick 20 H.P. Tonneau.*

Cyle and Automobile Trade Journal, October 1904, Hugh Dolnar, *The Buick Motor Company's Side Entrance Tonneau,* one of the best early account of Buick's beginnings, plus the first test ride of a Buick by a journalist.

Auto Trade Journal, October 1904, first Buick car ad.

The Motor World, November 24, 1904, *Buick Gets License,* explaining Buick took over the Selden license of Pope-Robinson and would therefore become a full-fledged member of the Association of Licensed Automobile Manufacturers.

The Motor World, undated, probably February 1905, a brief interview with David Buick on his engine while at New York Auto Show.

Cycle and Automobile Trade Journal, December 1905, *Buick Motor Brake Horse Power,* Hugh Dolnar defends his statements on Buick's power.

New York World, November 2, 1910, Buick Oil Company advertisement.

The Horseless Age, November 30, 1910, *Buick's Oil Venture Gets Black Eye.*

Los Angeles Times, January 27, 1912, *His Reward a Freeze-out?* Ralph Arnold's lawsuit against Buick Oil Company. There are several articles on Buick Oil Company in this newspaper in the 1910-15 period, including *Accusations in Rebuttal,* April 17, 1912, Benjamin F. Moffatt, who demands return of large block of Buick stock, is criticized by firm's secretary; *Busy Day for New Tribunal,* October 27, 1914, reference to Buick Oil Company case, and *Too Much of It,* April 23, 1915, judge criticizes complaint against Buick Oil Company.

Press Reference Library: Notables of the West, International News Service, Volume 1, 1913. David Buick biographical sketch.

Buick Weekly, March 19, 1920, *Beacraft Helped Make 'lst' Buick.*

Detroit Saturday Night, Benjamin Briscoe Jr., *The Inside Story of General Motors,* January 1921. An excellent historical account by one of David Buick's most important early associates.

Automotive Industries, June 1921, announcement on David Buick's design for a new car to be marketed as the Lorraine.

Buick Bulletin, October 1921, *Men You Should Know About: Walter L. Marr.*

Motor, January 1923, *That Man Durant,* W.A.P. John.

Automotive Industries, April 26, 1923, on David Buick's plans to build Dunbar automobile.

Newspaper Enterprise Association, April 28, 1928, Bruce Catton, *David Buick, Founder of Buick, Lives in Poverty at Age of 74.* This is the only extensive interview of David Buick by a professional journalist, a year before Buick's death.

National Cyclopedia of American Biography, David Buick, undated, but after David Buick's death in 1929.

The Buick Magazine, September 1937, *Buick in the Beginning.*

Chattanooga Free Press, October 5, 1937, Sam Adkins, *"Walter Marr Came Here to Die..."*

Old Timers News, August 1952, W.H. Wascher, *Buick and Mustachioed Workers Build a 'Better' Engine in 1904.* Memories of a worker who started at Buick in 1903.

Flint News-Advertiser, August 11, 1953, Ben Bennett, *Pine Yardstick, Piece of String,* early Flint Wagon Works workers reminisce about building first Flint Buick.

MacLean's, Oct. 1-Oct. 15, 1954, *My Eighty Years on Wheels,* by R.S. McLaughlin as told to Eric Hutton.

Elgin (Illinois) *Courier-News,* August 11, 1964, Edward F. Gathman, *Fire Wrote End to Elgin Car Manufacture Venture,* Last Marr Autocars go up in flames in August 1904.

Automobile Quarterly, Summer 1968, *Wouldn't You Really Rather be a Buick?,* Beverly Rae Kimes.

The Flint Journal, October 2, 1980, Lawrence R. Gustin, *Mr. Buick drives a Plymouth,* interview with grandson of David Buick.

Special Interest Autos, December 1980, Keith Marvin, *The Dunbar Deception: Was David Buick a schnook or a sharpie?*

The Flint Journal, August 9, 1981, Lawrence R. Gustin, *'The Thing': Michigan home of 1880s car can call itself first 'auto city.'* Tracking down the story of Thomas Clegg of Memphis, Michigan, and Michigan's first automobile – a steam-engine vehicle.

Automobile Quarterly, Summer 1993, Lawrence R. Gustin, *The Buick Flint Would Really Rather Have.* A 1905 Model C returns to Buick.

Antique Automobile, March-April 1995, Terry B. Dunham, *Cobwebs and Overhead Valves,* an account of work leading to the first Buick valve-in-head engine.

Buick Bugle, a publication of the Buick Club of America, December 2003, *Searching for Mr. Marr,* Terry B. Dunham.

Various newspaper articles in the Charles E. Hulse collection at Sloan Museum's Buick Gallery and Research Center are not listed separately. There are also others, some undated and unidentified as to source, in the files of William Close, Terry Dunham, Kevin Kirbitz and the author, as well as in the files of the Sloan Museum and its Buick Gallery and Research Center in Flint, Michigan.

Original letters, manuscripts and other documents from the estate of William C. Durant, first used by the author for his biography, *Billy Durant: Creator of General Motors,* in 1973 and since sold by Catherine L. Durant's estate to the General Motors Institute Foundation, are now in the Richard P. Scharchburg Archives at Kettering University in Flint. Additional Durant documents given later to the author by Aristo Scrobogna, Durant's last personal secretary, and by his daughter, Estelle Roberts, are now in the author's collection.

Birth record of David Buick in Arbroath, Scotland, are courtesy of Eric Buick of Arbroath. Eric Buick also provided information about David Buick's early life in Scotland.

Letters, Manuscrpits, Audio-Video

- Fred G. Hoelzle, manuscript, undated, discussing early role with Eugene Richard, Walter Marr and David Buick.

- Various letters between Walter Marr and several associates, including David Buick, author's collection.

- Michael W. R. Davis, master's thesis on Charles G. Annesley, author's collection.

- Legal depositions by W.C. Durant and James H. Whiting, 1911, author's collection. These were in response to a complaint by William S. Ballenger and other Buick stockholders that Whiting had reached a secret agreement with Durant in which Whiting would receive a substantial block of Buick stock after helping Durant sell a stockholders' agreement to the other shareholders. Durant and Whiting denied the charge, with Durant contending he did not decide until later that he needed Whiting's help to manage the company.

- Charles W. Nash, letter to Fred Warner, manager of Buick in Chicago, December 19, 1913, almost dismissing David Buick's role in the company's past. Buick Gallery and Research Center, Sloan Museum, Flint.

- Frank J. DeLaney, manuscript, *A History of the Buick Motor Company,* undated. Early employee relates history as he remembers it. Author's collection.

- Charles E. Hulse, hand-written notes on interview of Walter Marr, 1934. Author's collection. Copy in Hulse collection, Buick Gallery and Research Center, Sloan Museum, Flint.

- A.B.C. Hardy, recollections, 1946, Buick Gallery and Research Center, Sloan Museum, Flint.

- *Legend of Buick,* Buick Centennial DVD, Lawrence R. Gustin, director; Bill Harris, narrator; Buick Gallery and Research Center, Sloan Museum, Flint. Motion pictures of Walter Marr and other auto pioneers including Louis Chevrolet, Charles W. Nash and

Walter P. Chrysler; voice recording and brief motion pictures, William C. Durant. Includes video of David Buick birthplace commemoration, Arbroath, Scotland, 1994.

- R. Samuel McLaughlin, letter to Buick General Manager Ed Rollert, October 27, 1964, gives his version on how W.C. Durant first rode in a Buick (at least partly inaccurate). Author's collection.

- David Buick, letter to Walter Marr, December 11, 1913, discusses Marr's Cyclecar. Buick Gallery and Research Center, Sloan Museum, Flint.

- Buick Oil Company lawsuit documents dated 1914 and 1915 filed under Equity Case A121, National Archives and Records Administration, Laguna Niguel, Calif.

- Thomas D. Buick, letter to a boat manufacturer, J.C. Schmidt, October 21, 1903. Discusses Buick marine engines and the company's upcoming move to Flint. Terry B. Dunham Collection. Copy in *The Buick: A Complete History,* sixth edition.

- James J. Storrow, letter to Hugh G. Levick, Higginson & Company, London, England, September 24, 1915. Leroy Cole collection.

- Alvan Macauley, letter to U.S., Sen. Truman H. Newberry, December 19, 1919, author's collection.

Index

A

AC Spark Plug, 147
Adkins, Sam, 64
Afghanistan, 10
"Ainsley" (Annesley), Charles, 59
Albany, N.Y., 126
Aldrich, Fred A., 119, 127, 191
Alexander Manufacturing Co., 24, 25
American Gas automobile, 69, 70
American Heritage, 18
American Locomotive plant, 175
American Motor Carriage Co., 55-57, 69, 70, 72, 103, 104
Angus (Scotland) District Council, 190
Anker, Sam, 43, 50
Annesley, Charles G., 15, 45, 47, 49, 57-62
Antique Automobile, 63, 178, 186
Apperson brothers, 84
Arbroath Abbey, 23
Arbroath, Scotland, 21-23, 188-191
Armstrong, Bert, 105
Armstrong Spring and Axle Co., 105
Arnold, Delos, 167
Arnold, Horace, 118
Arnold, Ralph, 166-168
Around the World in 80 Days rally, 11
Auto Brass & Aluminum Co., 150, 151
The Automobile, 85, 86
Automotive Hall of Fame, 12, 191
Automotive Industries, 178

B

Bagley Avenue, Detroit, 45, 46
Barthel, Oliver, 47
Bassett, Harry H., 175
BBC, 188
Beacraft, William, 17, 98, 106, 139
Beadle, Rachel, 151
Beaubien Street, 14, 37
Beecroft, D., 86
Begole, Charles M., 91, 101, 114, 141
Begole, Fox & Co., 90
Bent, Don, 210
Bennett, Ben, 105
Bennett, Harry, 62
Benz automobiles, 32
Benz, Karl, 30
Bergman, Ingrid, 12
"Bewick" (Briscoe Buick), 86

Birmingham, Mich., 191
Bishop, Arthur G., 138
Bishop public school, 23
Boes, Doug, 39
Bogart, Humphrey, 12
Borden Milk plant (Walden, N.Y.), 179
Boston, 121, 150
Boydell Building, Detroit, 37
Briscoe, Benjamin Jr., 19, 69, 73, 81, 84-89, 96, 101, 102, 121, 146
"Briscoe Buick," 73, 84, 85, 86, 90
Briscoe, Frank, 89
Brooks, Pat, 11
Bryant House hotel, 109
Buffalo Gasolene Motor Co., 57, 61, 62
Buffalo, N.Y., 57, 62
Buick (Buik), Alexander, 21-23
Buick, Amy, 210
Buick Auto-Vim and Power Co., 37, 39, 43, 51, 52, 66, 67, 103, 188
Buick, Caroline Katherine (Schwinck), 26, 39, 181
Buick Club of America, 190
Buick, David Dunbar
    Birth, 21
    Early career, 24-27
    Marriage to Caroline, 26
    Plumbing business, 19, 26
    Start in gasoline engines, 29
    Relationship with Briscoe, 81-88
    Sells to Flint Wagon Works, 91
    Move to Flint, 137, 138
    Goes to California, 17, 153-174
    Interviewed by Catton, 17, 18
    Death, 183
Buick, David Dunbar II, 13, 19, 156, 157, 181
Buick, Eric G., 21, 22, 189, 191, 210
Buick, Frances Jane, 26, 138, 151, 164
Buick Gallery and Research Center, 15, 190, 191, 209, 230, 231
Buick (or Buik), Jane Rodger, 21
Buick, Mabel (or Maybelle) Lucille, 26, 138, 151, 164
Buick Manufacturing Co., 56, 68, 71, 83, 85, 98, 187
Buick, Margaret Harrington, 182, 183
Buick Midway Holdings, 162
Buick Models (concept cars)
    Y-Job, 9
    XP-300, 9

222

Index

LeSabre, 9
Centurion, 9
LeSabre, 9
Wildcat, 9
Velite, 9
Buick Models (experimental and production)
    First Buick, 52, 54
    First Flint Buick, 103-114
    1904 Model B, 51-56, 103-120
    1905 Model C, 134-147
    1906 Model G, 145
    1907 models D, H, S, K, 145
    1906-08 Model F, 145, 147
    1908-10 Model !0, 145, 147
    1908 Model 5, 79
    1909 Model 6, 79
    1909-1910 Model 41
    1925 Standard Model 25X, 10
    1940 Limited Phaeton, 12
    1948 Special, 10
    1949 Super Woody Wagon, 11
    1949 Roadmaster convertible, 12
    2002 Rendezvous, 11
    Century, 9
    Electra, 186
    GNX, 9
    Grand National, 9
    Gran Sport, 9
    Invicta, 186
    LeSabre, 9
    Park Avenue, 189
    Riviera, 9
    Skylark, 9
    Special, 9
    Super, 9
Buick Motor Co.,
    Incorporated, 83
    Sold to Flint Wagon Works directors, 91, 93
    General, 17, 64, 83, 88, 98, 101, 104, 113, 119, 135, 144, 153, 155, 160, 187
Buick Oil Association, 168-174
Buick Oil Co., 154-174
Buick Open golf tournament, 10
Buick production numbers (first years), 134
Buick, Sally, 213
Buick & Sherwood Manufacturing Co., 25, 35, 82, 108, 159
Buick Super Low Emission Vehicle (SULEV), 80
Buick, Thomas D., 96, 101, 109, 111, 114, 118, 136, 138, 150, 151, 181
Buicktown (Flint) Chapter, Buick Club of America, 190
Buick tri-shield crest, 186
Buick "White Streak" Model 10, 145

Buick, William Dunbar, 23, 213
Buick, William Wolcott, 23, 213
Buick, Wynton R., 26, 115, 183
Bulgari, Nicola, 12, 190, 230
Burke's Heraldry, 185
Burman, Bob, 10
Burns, Ken, 83
Burr Brothers, 165
Burr, Sheldon C., 165

C

Cadillac, Antoine de la Mothe, 26
Cadillac automobile, 98, 145
Calder, C. B., 38
California, 19, 130, 154, 155
California gold rush, 130
Calver, Bert, 105, 106
Carrie B., 39
Carton, John J., 138, 139, 151, 152, 154
Casablanca, 12
Case, Alfred E., 167-173
Cass Avenue, 52
Catton, Bruce, 17-20, 153, 155, 157, 182, 191,192
Champion, Albert, 147
Champlain Street, Detroit, 37
Charlotte, Mich., 107
Chattanooga Free Press, 64
Chevrolet, Arthur, 148
Chevrolet "bow tie" logo, 149
Chevrolet-Buick Freeway, 187
Chevrolet, Louis, 10, 148, 153, 187
Chevrolet Motor Co., 148
Chicago, 23, 91, 117, 119,121, 150
Chicago Times-Herald auto race, 30, 32
Chicago World's Fair, 30, 33
China, 10
Chrysler, Walter P., 12, 175, 176, 181
Chrysler Corp.,
Cigar-making, 130
Citizens National Bank, 121
The City of Flint Grows Up, 138
Civil War, 24, 137
Clegg, John, 29
Clegg, Tom, 29, 30
Cleveland, Ohio, 56, 69, 70, 103
Close, Sarah, 52, 209, 211
Close, William B., 15, 47, 52, 62, 74, 209, 211
Cobe Trophy, 153
Cofield engine, 47
Coldwater Road Cart Co., 121
Coletta, Robert E., 189
Cologne, Germany, 22
Continental engine, 180

223

David Buick's Marvelous Motor Car

Cornell University, 77
Cortez, 102
Cotharin, George V., 108
Coyle, James D., Realty, 164
Coyle, James Duryea, 164
Crapo, Henry Howland, 92
Crawford, Kim, 212
Crimean War, 22
Crow, Carl, 102, 138
Crowther, Samuel, 60
Cruise, Tom, 12
Cumings, Charles A., 90
Curtice, Harlow H., 12
Cycle and Automobile Trade Journal, 51, 97

D

David Buick Carburetor Co., 181, 182
David Dunbar Buick Corp., 179
Davis, Michael W. R., 15, 60, 62, 210
Davis, William F., 74, 77
Dearborn, Mich., 33, 191
DeCou, Jack, 212
Deere, John, 77
DeLaney, Frank J., 65
Del Prado Hotel, 32
Detroit, 17, 18, 19, 23, 26, 29, 37, 45, 48, 51, 52, 56, 70, 71, 91, 104, 108, 109, 110, 117, 134, 150, 188, 190
Detroit Athletic Club, 62
Detroit Brass, Iron and Novelty Co., 56
Detroit Free Press, 23
Detroit Journal, 33
Detroit News, 66, *154*
Detroit Press Club, 187
Detroit River, 23, 41, 42
Detroit School of Trades, 18, 182
Detroit Shipbuilding Co., 38, 39
Detroit Tribune, 5, 59
Detroit Yacht Club, 39
DeWaters, Enos A., 19, 145, 175, 177
Dixon, Michael, 210, 212
Dolnar, Hugh, 52, 53, 114-119
Dolson automobile, 107
Dornbos, J.L., 179
Dort, Josiah Dallas, 121-124, 127
Dresden Hotel, 146
Dullan, Jannie, 138
Duluth, Minn., 23
Dunbar automobile, 178-182
Duncan, Dayton, 83
Dunham, Terry B., 14, 15, 63, 68, 69, 73, 153, 209
du Pont, Pierre, 177
Durant, Catherine, 13, 149
Durant, Clara, 134

Durant-Dort Carriage Co., 93, 111, 119, 123, 124, 127, 141
Durant-Dort Headquarters (National Historic Site), 191
Durant horse barn, 191
Durant, Margery, 126, 148
Durant, William C., 13, 14, 17, 64, 65, 80, 121-154, 157, 158, 169, 175, 176, 177, 183, 188, 191, 192
Duryea, Charles and Frank, 30, 32

E

Eagle Rock, 135
Earl, Harley, 185
Eastern Michigan University, 60
East Tawas, Mich., 43
Eddy, Arthur Jerome, 126
Edison Illuminating Co., 33, 49
Edward VIII, King of England, 10
Elges, George, 186, 187
Elgin, Ill, 73
En-lai, Zhou, 10

F

Fairbanks, Charles V. (U.S. vice president), 138
"Famous Blue Ribbon Line," 134
Fauber Manufacturing Co., 73
Fauth, G. Gregory, 187, 210
Fenton, Miss., 138
Ferris, George, 178
Ferris Wheel, 30
Flanders, Francis, 108
Flint Daily News, 108, 117, 144
"Flint Flyer" 1910 aircraft, 177
Flint Gas Light Co., 131
The Flint Journal, 93, 98, 109, 111, 150
Flint, Mich., 13, 15, 89-107, 113, 120, 132, 134, 141, 150, 159, 164, 165, 169, 176-178, 181, 187-189, 190, 191
Flint News-Advertiser, 105, 116
Flint Road Cart Co., 123, 191
Flint (Hardy Flint) Roadster, 90
Flint Wagon Works, 89-93, 101, 108, 111
Florida, 174
Flower, James & Brothers, 24, 25, 49
Fogelson, George J., 212
Ford, Clara, 48
Ford, Model T, 60, 145
Ford, Henry, 15, 19, 30, 33, 45, 46, 48, 49, 57, 58, 59, 62, 145, 146, 147, 148, 192
France, 155, 182
Franklin automobile, 65, 69, 73
Franklin, David, 211

224

Index

Franklin, Herbert H., 65, 77, 115
Franklin, H.H., Manufacturing Co., 65
Fries, Harold, 29, 30
Frigidaire, 149

G

Gardner, Ernest, 191, 211
Gardner, Janet, 211
The Gasoline Age, 145
General Motors, 9, 13-15, 27, 57, 132, 153, 159, 176, 177, 181, 185, 188, 192
General Motors Building, 187
General Motors of Canada, 10
General Motors World Headquarters, 188
General Motors Export, 10
Genesee Tire Co., 151
Glasgow Sunday Post, 186
Glasscock, C.B., 145
GMC Truck, 147
Gold mining, 164
Golden Jubilee of Flint, 138, 152
Golf and Buick, 10
Grand Rapids, Mich., 178, 189
Grand River Avenue, 45, 46, 52, 59
Great Britain, 188
Green, Fitzhugh, 149
Green Street, 21
Gregor, William 134
Gritzinger, Bob, 212
Grosse Pointe, Mich., 114
Gustin, Edward M., 213

H

Hall, E.J., 79
Hall-Scott Motor Co., 79
Hantak, Frank, 210
Hardy, A.B.C. (Alexander Brownell Cullen), 90, 92, 124, 126, 154, 155, 157
Hardy, Flint Roadster, 90
Harper Hospital, 183
Harrington, Margaret, 182, 183
Harroun, Ray, 66
Hastings, Henry J., funeral rooms, 183
Haynes automobile, 178
Haynes, Elwood, 84
Hays, Joan, 211
Hercules engine, 45
Herndon, John M., 162
Highland Park Plant, 60
Hills, Herbert H., 116, 117, 126-130
Historical Crossroads Village, 191
Hoeft, Harry H., 179
Hoelzle, Fred G., 13, 98, 99, 152

Hoffman, Dustin, 12
Holmes, Margaret G., 212
Homans, James E., 78
Horatio's Drive, 83
The Horseless Age, 166
Hough, Arthur W., 104, 105
Howard, Charles, 148
Howard Street, 56, 95, 187
Howarth, J.B., 95
Hulse, Charles E., 14, 15, 48, 68, 70, 73, 85, 86, 97, 107, 111, 113, 187, 209
Hutton, Eric, 129
Hyde, Charles K., 212
Hygienic Seat Co., 37

I

The Implement Age, 115
Inca Trail adventure drive, 11, 12
Indianapolis 500, 10
Indians, 91
Irving, Thomas E., 213

J

Jackson automobile, 107
Jackson Carburetor Co., 182
Jackson, Horatio Nelson, 83
Jackson, Mich., 107, 134, 141-145
Janney Motor Co., 145
Janney, P.R., 145
Jefferson Avenue, 15
Jeffery, Thomas B., Co., 176
Johnson, Donald E., 128
Johnson, Gerald, 187
Johnson, Jim, 187
Johore, sultan of, 177
Jump spark ignition, 51, 52

K

Kaufman, Ken, 149
Kearsley Street, East, 117, 138
Kearsley Street, West, 93
Kelley, Susan, 15, 209
Kern County, Calif., 162
Kimes, Beverly Rae, 186
King, Charles Brady, 30, 45, 47, 49, 58, 60, 61
King of England (Edward VIII), 10
King, Stephen, 12
Kirbitz, Kevin M., 52, 74-76, 210
Kleptz, Chic, 211
Klug, Tom, 212
Kneeland, C.L., 96
Kneeland Crystal Creamery, 66, 95, 98

Kneeland, Sarah, 96
Koehler, H. J., 135
Kokomo, Ind., 178
Kulick, Frank (Ford 999 driver), 115
Kutz, J., 183
Kyles, George, 172, 173

L

Lafayette Street (Detroit), 37
Lake Erie, 23
Lake Huron, 43
Lake St. Clair, 23
Lamb, Stacy C., 162
Lansing, Mich., 96
Lapeer, Mich., 109, 111, 187
Larkin, John H., 178
Lehigh, J.B., 162, 169
Lewis, David L., 48, 212
Lexington, Mich., 43
Libby Prison, 137
Liberty engine, 79
Lincoln, Abraham, 24, 92
Little, Big Bill, 160
Little Egypt, 30
Locomobile, 76
Lodge, John C., 19
Lorraine Motor Corp., 178
Los Angeles, 154, 159, 161, 164, 190
Los Angeles Times, 162
Lumbering, 130

M

Macauley, Alvan, 176
MacLean's magazine, 129
Maines, George H., 14, 157
Marmon automobile, 66, 77
Marmon, Howard, 66, 77
Marmon Wasp, 66
Marquette, Mich., 23
Marquette (Buick) automobile, 79
Marr, Abbie, 52
Marr Autocar, 71, 73, 209
Marr Cyclecar, 171
Marr Field, 178
Marr, George Ernest, 43
Marr motor tricycle, 51, 69
Marr, Richard A., 211
Marr, Walter L., 14
    Birth, 43
    Early life, 43
    Early career, 39
    Manager at Buick Auto-Vim, 40, 41
    First gasoline engine, 43

Bicycle shop, 45, 46
Talks with Henry Ford, 45, 47
Motor tricycle, 51, 69
First Buick, 51, 52
Leaves Buick first time, 54
Friendship with Charles Annesley, 57-62
With valve-in-head engine, 63
With American Motor Carriage Co., 69
With Reid Co.'s Wolverine automobile, 97
Return to Buick, 103-120
Persuades Whiting to build cars, 104
Driving Flint Buick, 108-111
Marr, Walter L. III, 211
Marvin, Keith, 179, 180
Mason, Arthur C., 98, 114, 115, 136, 139, 144
Maxwell automobile, 84, 87
Maxwell-Briscoe Co., 84, 146
Maxwell, Jonathan D., 84, 87
May, George S., 13, 47, 55, 59-61
McCosh, Dan, 212
McCreery, Col. William, 137
McLaughlin, Sam, 129, 130
Melbourne, Australia 22
Meldrum Avenue, 26, 103, 138
Memphis, Mich., 29, 30
Mexican Petroleum Co., 167
Meyer, Dennis 190
Michigan historical markers, 188, 191
Milne, Brian, 190
Minchener, Charlotte, 60
Minden, Neb., 190
Miner, John M., 167, 169, 172
Moessner, Emil D., 83
Moffatt, Benjamin F., 168
Montreal, 126
Montrose, Scotland, 22
A Most Unique Machine, 13
Motor City, 32
Motor Trend, 9
The Motor World, 135, 136
Motor Vehicle Review, 35
Mott, Charles Stewart, 13, 176, 177
Mueller-Benz automobile, 32
Mueller, Hieronymus, 32
Mueller, Oscar, 32
Murray, W. S., 36, 38-40
My Life and Work, 59

N

Napolean III, 22
Nash, Charles W., 171-173, 175, 176
Newark, N.J., 135
Newberry, U.S. Sen. Truman H., 177
New Hampshire, 83

Index

Newmark, Jacob H., 87, 88
New York, 22, 119
New York Auto Show 1905, 134, 135
New York Herald, 154
New York Times, 165
Noeker, Joseph, 55, 56

O

Oakland automobile, 147, 147, 176
Oldsmobile automobile, 76, 103, 104
Oldsmobile Detroit plant, 55, 66
Oldsmobile engine, 47
Oldsmobile, Ransom E., 30, 33, 84, 146, 147
O'Leary, Howard, 185
Olson, Sidney, 25, 46
Orrell, Lucy Crapo, 126
Orrell, William C., 107
Otto, Nikolaus August, 34
Overhead-valve engine, 56, 63-81
Owosso, Mich., 150

P

Packard Motor Car Co., 78, 176
Panhard automobile, 126
Parkhill, James 105
S. Pasadena, Calif., 162
Paterson, Will, 107
Paterson, William A., 107, 123
Paterson, William A., Carriage Works, 93
Patrick, Mark, 212
Patterson, Caroline Louisa, 164
Patterson, Frank C., 183
Pearl Harbor, 12
Peck, Barton, 45, 48, 49, 61
Peerless Motor Co., 96, 98, 101
Peking to Paris rally, 10, 11
Penobscot Building, 146
Perry, Mich., 104
Pew, Ralph, 185
Philadelphia, 66
Pioneer Village, 190
Plymouth automobile, 181
Pontchartrain Hotel (old), 146
Pontiac, Mich., 90
Pope-Robinson Co.,132
Port Huron, Mich., 29
Pound, Arthur, 27, 29, 36, 69, 122, 123, 154
Public Image of Henry Ford, 48

Q

Qingxiang, Wang, 177
"Quadricycle," (Henry Ford's), 32, 33, 48, 57.
Quay, Charles, 111, 132

R

Ragsdale, Edward T., 185
Reddy, T. M., 165
"Red Devils," 107-108
Reid, Charles, 32
Reid engine, 97, 103
Reid Manufacturing Co., 97, 103
Renaissance Center, 188
Reno, Nev., 190
REO Motor Car Co., 46
Reuss, Lloyd E., 12
Richard, Eugene C., 66-69, 73, 75, 76, 83, 84, 95-101, 178, 192
Richard, Eugene D., 68
Rideout, Jerry, 187, 188
Rio de Janeiro, 12
The Road to Perdition, 12
Roberts, Estelle, 209
Rochester, N.Y., 66
Rodolf, Frank M., 211
Rodger, Jane, 21
Rollert, Ed, 29, 130
Rose, Walter, 162
Rough Riders, Teddy Roosevelt's, 148
Ryder Cup, 191

S

St. Andrew's Place, 164
St. Louis, Mo., 108
Saginaw, 43, 44
Saginaw Street, 105, 111
Saginaw Valley, 91
San Joaquin Geological Society, 162
Saratoga Springs, N.Y., 190
Sault Ste. Marie, 23
Savoy, France, 66
Schneider, J.P., 73
Schwinck, Caroline Katherine, 26, 39, 181
Scientific American, 33
Scotland, 14, 21-23, 188-190
Scrobogna, Aristo, 14, 209
Second Avenue, Detroit, 45, 59
Selden, George B., 132
Selden patent, 132
Shamrock oil gusher, 162
Self Propelled Vehicles, 78
Shanghai, 10
Shannon, Steve, 7, 8
Sherman, Don, 212
Sherwood Brass Co., 36
Sherwood, William, 25, 36, 54
Shickles, Tim, 191, 210
Signal Mountain, Tenn., 177

227

"Simmons," 136
Simpson, Mrs. Wallace, 10
Sintz engine, 45
Skaff, Jack, 15, 187, 210
Sloan, Alfred P. Jr., 9, 177
Sloan Museum, 15, 181, 187, 190, 191, 209, 230, 231
Smith, Flint P., 138, 152
Smith, Fred, 148
Sommer automobile, 107
South America, 10
Soviet Union, 10
Spark advance, 51, 52
Special Interest Autos, 179
Springfield, Mass., 30
Standard Oil Co., 162
Standard Sanitary Manufacturing Co., 36
Stanford University, 167
Stegmeyer, Albert, 41, 42, 44
Stevens-Duryea, 76
Stevens Street, 138
Stewart, W.F., Co., 93, 105
Stone, Dwight, 89
Storrow, James J., 175, 176
The Strand Magazine, 159
Strauss, Frederick, 24, 25
Sutherland, Alasdair M., 22
Syracuse, N.Y., 65

T

Taylor, Jeff, 210
"The Thing," 29, 30
Thomas automobile, 108
Thomas Flyer, 108
Thomas, Lowell, 10
Tiedeman, Fred, 97
Time, 184
de Tocqueville, Alexis, 91
Todd, John, 91
Todd, Polly, 91
Todd's Tavern, 91
Trinc, the bear, 91
Tucker Torpedo, 65
Tuolumne County, Calif., 164
The Turning Wheel, 27, 69, 130
Two Thousand Miles on an Automobile, 126

U

UAW Freeway, 187
Union Oil Co., 167
University Club, San Francisco, 83
U.S. Bicentennial, 187
U.S. Geological Survey, 167

V

Valve-in-head engine, 56, 63-81
Van Bolt, Roger, 14, 187
Van Noord, Roger, 212
Van Orman, Fred, 168, 169
"Vehicle City," 92, 93
Vincent, J.G., 79

W

Walden *Citizen-Herald,* 180
Walden, N.Y., 179, 180
Walker, George L., 91, 101
Walker, John, 43
Warm Springs, Va., 149
Warp, Harold, 190
Wascher, William H., 97
Waterloo Boy tractor, 77
Watson, Harry W., 108
Wayne automobile, 107
Western, S., Avenue, 164
Westinghouse Engine Co., 38
Whaley, Robert J., 121
Whiting, James, 89-93, 101, 104, 108, 113, 119, 121, 131, 138
Wicks Brothers, 43
Wildanger, William, 108
Wilkinson, John, 65, 68, 75, 77
Williams, Dan N., 211
Wilson, Daniel, 24
Winchester, W. F., 115
Winton automobile, 108
Wisconsin fair, 123
Wisner, Judge Charles, 92
Wolverine automobile, 97, 103
Wolverine Citizen, 106
Wolyn, A.H., 172, 173
Woodmere Cemetery, 183
Woods, Tiger, 10
Woodward Avenue, 32
World's Columbian Exposition, 18, 30, 93
Wyatt, A.H., 178

Y

Yatsen, Sun, 177
Yi, Pu, 10, 177
Young, Clarence H., 14
Young Henry Ford, 25, 48

Photo Index
(color photos in bold face)

A
American Gas automobile, 71
Annesley, Charles G., 61

B
Ballard, Anne, **203**
Barthel, Oliver, 31
Beacraft, William, 110, 123, 179
Begole, Charles, 115
Boes, Doug, **204**
Bower, Ferdinand (Dutch), 179
Boydell Building, 37, **193**
Briscoe, Benjamin, 85
"Briscoe Buick," 87
Buick advertising, 34, 133
Buick barn, 35
Buick, David drafting set, **203**
Buick, David Dunbar, 11, 18, 19, 22 (birth record), 106, 119, 155, 182, 186
Buick, David, letters, 50, 53, 107
Buick, Eric, 189
Buick Gallery and Research Center, **208**
Buick headquarters, **200, 202, 207**
Buick, Mabel Lucille (driving Model C), 139
Buick Manufacturing Co. catalog, **196**
Buick Manufacturing Co. engine, **193**
Buick, Margaret (Harrington), 182
Buick Models
    First Model B (stripped), 112, **195**, (replica **196**)
    1904 Model B, 115, 116, 129
    1905 Model C, 117, 131, 135, 139, **197**
    1908-10 Model 10, 146
    1953 Skylark, **208**
    1999 LeSabre, **196**
    2005 LaCrosse, **208**
Buick Motor Co. engine works, 110
Buick north Flint complex, 157, **199-202**
Buick Oil Co., 160, 161, 163
Buick & Sherwood, 25
Buick, Thomas, 112, 115
Buick W. Kearsley (Flint) plant, 127
Bulgari, Nicola, **206**

C
Chrysler, Walter, 170
Close, Barton, **194**
Close, Cindy, **194**
Close, Sarah, **194, 203**
Close, William B., **194**
Coletta, Robert, 189, **205**
Cyclecar, 170, **203**

D
DeCou, Jack, **205**

Dort, J. Dallas, 125
Dresden Hotel, **202**
Durant, Catherine, 124, 151
Durant-Dort Carriage Co. headquarters, 125
Durant, Margery (in Model C), 131
Durant, William C., 100, 122, 124, 125, 143

F
Fauth, G. Gregory, **206**
Flint, 94, 128, 129, 139, **198**
Flint Wagon Works, 96, **198**
Ford, Henry, 31

G
Green Street, Arbroath, Scotland, 24
Gustin, Lawrence R., 189

H
Hardy, A.B.C., 124
Hough, Arthur W., 109
Hulse, Charles E., 99

J
Jackson Buick factory, **198**
Jackson, Mich., 135, **199**

K
King, Charles B., 31

L
Lutz, Robert A., **208**

M
Marr, Abbie, 49, **194**
Marr, Richard, **203**
Marr, Walter (Skip) III, **203**
Marr Autocar, 72, **194**
Marr, Walter L., 40, 41, 44, 46, 49, 106, 112, 115, 119, 170, **194**
Mason, Arthur C., 100
Mertz, Edward M., **205**
Milne, Brian, 189, **205**

N
Nash, Charles W., 170

R
Renaissance Center, Detroit, **207**
Richard, Eugene C., 67, 88, 179
Richard, Louisa, 67, 88

S
Sherwood, William, 36

V
Valve-in-head engine, 28, 80, 100, **197**

W
Wascher, William H., 99
Whiting, James H., 92, 115
Williams, Joan, **203**

Buick Gallery and Research Center, Alfred P. Sloan Museum, Flint, Mich.

The Buick Gallery and Research Center of the Alfred P. Sloan Museum in Flint, Mich., was dedicated November 10, 1998, in a ceremony headed by Steve Germann, then director of the museum, and Robert E. Coletta, then Buick general manager and a General Motors vice president. The Gallery was designed to be a living legacy of Buick operations that had been headquartered in Flint since 1903, as well as a repository for Buick artifacts, photographs, documents and other papers. Buick's main office was being moved late in 1998 to join other GM marketing divisions at the corporation's world headquarters in Detroit's Renaissance Center.

"The Buick Gallery is a stake in the ground that makes a forceful statement that Buick and Flint will always be together," Coletta said at the ceremony. "It is one thing to say the heart and soul of Buick is in Flint – for many people that will always be true – but another to have a facility you can touch and tour...to remind future generations that this company and this city together stood for something very important.

"Together, the city and the company helped create a great industry. It was an industry that changed the way people live and brought both mobility and undreamed financial rewards to workers throughout the 20th Century."

Coletta said he hoped the Gallery would continue to grow, to "help researchers tell the story of Buick and Flint, to help restorers preserve the great Buicks of the past and to be a link that always ties Buick headquarters to Flint."

Today, the Sloan Museum and Buick Gallery together house one of the world's best Buick collections. About 40 vintage Buicks are displayed, including two 1905 Model Cs, the famous 1910 Buick Bug racer, the 1951 XP-300, 1954 Wildcat II and 1956 Centurion concept cars and even a World War II Buick-built Hellcat Tank Destroyer. Several well-restored Buicks from the late 1930s and early '40s, as well as model Buicks, have been donated to the Gallery in recent years by Nicola Bulgari, international jeweler and holder of one of the world's largest private Buick collections.

A replica – created by museum staff and volunteers – of the stripped 1904 Model B, first Buick built in Flint, is powered by a rare original 1904 Buick Model B engine, in working condition. Also displayed are horse carts built by the Coldwater Road Cart Company and Flint Road Cart Company, the products that brought William C. Durant into the vehicle business – the

Officials of the Alfred P. Sloan Museum and its Buick Gallery and Research Center (background) in Flint, Mich., admire a 1905 Buick Model C. They are Jeff Taylor (left), assistant director, and Tim Shickles, director. The car was once owned by Fred Aldrich, who helped persuade Billy Durant to take control of Buick Motor Company, leading to the creation of General Motors. The car, displayed in the Buick Gallery, is one of the oldest surviving Buicks; it has been in Flint for more than 100 years.

first vehicles in his career that resulted in the creation of General Motors. Among other artifacts is the personal drafting set of David Buick.

One of the 1905 Buicks, restored in 2003-2005 as a Buick centennial project, has been in Flint since it was delivered new to Fred Aldrich, secretary of the Durant-Dort Carriage Company, in 1905. Aldrich helped persuade Durant to take control of Buick in 1904.

Inquiries about the collection and contributions of artifacts (including vehicles), photographs and documents should go to Jeff Taylor, curator of collections, at (810) 237-3435. Financial contributions to support preserving Buick history and the maintenance of the museum's automobile collection may be directed to Tim Shickles, director of the museum and Buick Gallery. The main address is Sloan Museum, 1221 E. Kearsley Street, Flint, Mich., 48503.